<u>INDEX</u>

<u>Chapter One</u>

<u>Chapter Two</u>

Chapter One

Mossad Covert War

Mossad: Back in 2007

In an August 17 (2007) meeting, Israeli Mossad Chief Meir Dagan thanked Under Secretary Burns for America's support of Israel as evidenced by the previous day's signing of an MOU that provides Israel with USD 30 billion in security assistance from 2008-2018.

Dagan reviewed Israel's five-pillar strategy concerning Iran's nuclear program, stressed that Iran is economically vulnerable, and pressed for more activity with Iran's minority groups aimed at regime change.

Assessing the region, Dagan said Israel sees itself in the middle of a rapidly changing environment, in which the fate of one Middle Eastern country is connected to another. Turning to Iran, Dagan observed that it is in a transition period. Instability in Iran is driven by inflation and tension among ethnic minorities.

Dagan said that the Gulf states and Saudi Arabia are concerned about the growing importance of Iran and its influence on them. They are taking precautions, trying to increase their own military defensive capabilities. Referring to the Gulf Security Dialogue (GSD), Dagan warned that these countries would not be able to cope with the amount of weapons systems they intend to acquire: "They do not use the weapons effectively."

Turning to the Gulf Security Dialogue (GSD), Dagan said that enhancing the capabilities of the Gulf states "is the right direction to go," especially as they are afraid of Iran. Such a U.S. commitment will be a stabilizing factor in the region. Dagan clarified that he would not oppose U.S. security assistance to

America's Arab partners. He expressed concern, nevertheless, about the current policies of those partners — especially with regards to Syria and Iran. Dagan added that if those countries must choose between buying defensive systems from the U.S. or France, then he would prefer they buy systems from the U.S., as this would bring them closer to the U.S.

Five Pillar Strategy

Dagan led discussion on Iran by pointing out that the U.S. and Israel have different timetables concerning when Iran is likely to acquire a nuclear capability. He clarified that the Israel Atomic Energy Commission's (IAEC) timetable is purely technical in nature, while the Mossad considers other factors, including the regime's determination to succeed. While Dagan acknowledged that there is still time to "resolve" the Iran nuclear crisis, he stressed that Iran is making a great effort to achieve a nuclear capability: "The threat is obvious, even if we have a different timetable. If we want to postpone their acquisition of a nuclear capability, then we have to invest time and effort ourselves."

Dagan described how the Israeli strategy consists of five pillars:

A) *Political Approach*: Dagan praised efforts to bring Iran before the UNSC, and signaled his agreement with the pursuit of a third sanctions resolution. He acknowledged that pressure on Iran is building up, but said this approach alone will not resolve the crisis. He stressed that the timetable for political action is different than the nuclear project's timetable.

B) *Covert Measures*: Dagan and the Under Secretary agreed not to discuss this approach in the larger group setting.

C) *Counter-proliferation*: Dagan underscored the need to prevent know-how and technology from making their way to Iran, and said that more can be done in this area.

D) *Sanctions*: Dagan said that the biggest successes had so far been in this area. Three Iranian banks are on the verge of collapse. The financial sanctions are having a nationwide impact. Iran's regime can no longer just deal with the bankers themselves.

E) *Force Regime Change*: Dagan said that more should be done to foment regime change in Iran, possibly with the support of student democracy movements, and ethnic groups (e.g., Azeris, Kurds, Baluchs) opposed to the ruling regime.

Dagan clarified that the U.S., Israel and like-minded countries must push on all five pillars at the same time. Some are bearing fruit now; others would bear fruit in due time, especially if more attention were placed on them. Dagan urged more attention on regime change, asserting that more could be done to develop the identities of ethnic minorities in Iran. He said he was sure that Israel and the U.S. could "change the ruling regime in Iran, and its attitude towards backing terror regimes." He added, "We could also get them to delay their nuclear project. Iran could become a normal state."

Dagan stressed that Iran has weak spots that can be exploited. According to his information, unemployment exceeds 30 percent nationwide, with some towns and villages experiencing 50 percent unemployment, especially among 17-30 year olds. Inflation averages more than 40 percent, and people are criticizing the government for investing in and sponsoring Hamas, saying that they government should invest in Iran itself. "The economy is hurting," he said, "and this is provoking a real crisis among Iran's leaders." He added that Iran's minorities are "raising their heads, and are tempted to resort to violence."

Dagan suggested that more could be done to get the Europeans to take a tougher stand against Iran. Under Secretary Burns agreed, and suggested that Israel could help by reaching out to the Europeans. Dagan said that Israel is already doing this, and would continue to do so. Dagan reiterated the need to strike at Iran's heart by engaging with its people directly.

Voice of America (VOA) broadcasts are important, but more radio transmissions in Farsi are needed. Coordination with the Gulf states is helpful, but the U.S. should also coordinate with Azerbaijan and countries to the north of Iran, to put pressure on Iran. Russia, he said, would be annoyed, but it would be fitting, as Russia appears bent on showing the U.S. that it cannot act globally without considering Russia.

Under Secretary Burns stressed that the USG is focused on Iran not only because of its nuclear program, but also because it supports terrorism and Shiite militias in Iraq. The U.S. approach is currently focused on the diplomatic track and increasing pressure on Iran through sanctions. Work in the UNSC helps to define the Iranian nuclear threat as one that affects international security, and not just that of Israel.

While UNSC members Russia, China and Qatar will water down efforts to increase pressure on Iran, it is still worthwhile to push for a third sanctions resolution. In the meantime, the U.S. will encourage the Europeans, Japan and South Korea to implement unilateral sanctions against Iran outside the UNSC framework. The U.S. will continue to encourage banks and financial institutions to slow down their operations in Iran and financially isolate it.

Regarding military pressure, the Under Secretary noted that the U.S. has deployed 1-2 carrier battle groups in the Gulf over the last six months, and that President Bush has stated that he will interrupt Iran's activity in Iraq. As for outreach to the Iranian people, the VOA is now broadcasting programs in Farsi, and the USG is trying to get more Iranian students to visit the U.S. to promote people-to-people relations.

Iran's counter intelligence

In its ongoing shadow war with Israel, the Iranian side's lone "success" was the July 18 bombing of a Bulgarian bus carrying Israeli tourists — though European investigators last week officially attributed that attack to Iran's Lebanese proxy, Hizballah. That leaves the Islamic Republic itself with a failure rate hovering near 100% abroad and an operational tempo — nine overseas plots uncovered in nine months — that carries a whiff of desperation. A Tehran government long branded by U.S. officials as the globe's leading exporter of terrorism may be cornering the market on haplessness.

Within Iran's own borders, however, the story is different. Twice in the past two years Iranian intelligence has cracked espionage rings working with Israel's Mossad. In both cases, the arrests were the furthest thing from secret: announced at a news conference, each was later followed up by televised confessions broadcast on Iranian state television in prime time. Given Iran's history of trumped-up confessions, skepticism is more than justified. But the arrests appear to be solid. One intelligence official said the captured Iranians provided "support and logistics" to the Mossad operatives who carried out the assassinations of Iranian nuclear scientists.

At least four scientists were killed on Tehran's streets from 2010 to 2012, when Israel ratcheted back on covert operations inside Iran. Officially, Israel has remained silent on the killings, though government officials will coyly say they welcome the deaths. The Jewish state maintains the same ambiguous posture on other "setbacks" to Iran's nuclear program widely — and correctly, Western intelligence officials say — attributed to Mossad, from the Stuxnet computer virus, to mysterious explosions like the massive blast at a missile base, which destroyed ballistic missiles that could reach Israel.

The covert onslaught dovetails with Israel's history of reaching "over the horizon" to disarm perceived threats at a distance. To keep advanced arms from reaching Hamas and Hizballah, Israel in the past year sent warplanes to bomb convoys and arms depots in Sudan and Syria, respectively, without apparent retribution. In the case of Iran, however, experts say the audacity of Israel's covert campaign stirred Tehran to revive an espionage effort that lay largely fallow since 9/11. The *Spy vs. Spy* contest that ensued would prove woefully one-sided, even in the third-world countries where Iran chose to strike, hoping to avoid heightened security awareness in the developed world. In the end, its only success came inside Iran, where the secret police operate without inhibition.

Mossad 's killings

The shadow war may have started on Jan. 15, 2007, the day Ardeshir Hosseinpour passed away. Hosseinpour was a specialist in electromagnetics at the Nuclear Technology Center in the city of Isfahan, Iran, but his death might have escaped notice had Iran's government not kept it under wraps for almost a week, finally attributing it to fumes from a faulty heater. An online report by the American private intelligence firm Stratfor suggested another cause — radioactive poisoning — and hinted that Mossad's Caesarea section was back in business.

Caesarea, named for an Israeli beach town that dates back to Roman times, is the operations branch of Israel's secret service, most notoriously responsible for the assassinations of some two dozen Palestinians (and an innocent waiter) after the 1972 Munich Olympics. Assassinations are carried out by a very small unit dubbed Kidon, the Hebrew word for "tip of the spear." Kidon operates at a remove from the legions of Mossad employees working in less lethal fields.

It would have been a unit called Hatzomet, or "The Junction," that recruited Majid Fashi, a handsome young Iranian who dropped out of high school to pursue a career in kickboxing. By the account he gave on Iranian state television early in 2011, Fashi presented himself at the Israeli consulate in Istanbul in 2007 and was vetted for a solid year before being shown any trust. Two years later, on Jan. 12, 2010, he would place a bomb on a motorbike parked on the sidewalk outside the Tehran home of Masoud Ali Mohammadi; the nuclear physicist was killed when it was detonated by remote control.

In the broadcast, Fashi accurately described the Mossad campus north of Tel Aviv. He said he had been given a laptop equipped with a second operating system and used it to communicate through online drop boxes. He was impressed by his handlers' thoroughness. At one point Fashi described studying a scale model of Ali Mohammadi's street. "It was an exact copy of the real one," Fashi said. "The tree next it, the street curb, the bridge." In a later broadcast, he was seated across from Ali Mohammadi's widow, who glared at him as he bowed his head and wept. Mossad officials were "pissed off and shocked" seeing their agent on television, the intelligence official said.

Fashi was executed in May 2012. About the same time, Iran's intelligence minister announced the arrest of 14 more Iranians, eight men and six women dubbed members of the "Terror Club" in the subsequent prime-time broadcast of that name. Filmed in shadow, and rich in atmospherics, the Aug. 5 program recreated Ali mohammadi's death and four subsequent attacks: they started with the Nov. 29, 2010 nearly simultaneous attempts on Majid Shariari and Fereydoun Abbasi, nuclear scientists driving to work when magnetic "sticky bombs" were attached to the side of their cars from passing motorcycles. Abbasi managed to escape before it detonated, saving his wife as well. Shariari was killed — a significant setback for the Iranian nuclear program where he was the top scientist, according to a Western intelligence official.

The confessed agents offered absorbing detail — they were aboard a Bajaj Pulsar, wearing helmets, when the magnet bomb stuck on the right front panel of Shariari's car exploded. The riders scrambled into the "trail car" assigned to follow the target and disappeared into the traffic of the Imam Ali Autobahn. Already gone was the car assigned to cut off and slow the car carrying the scientist. They claimed to have rehearsed on a practice track inside Israel. None of the details could be confirmed, but an intelligence official acknowledged: "Another network was taken."

The third scientist, Dariush Rezaeinejad was shot on July 23, 2011 after picking up his child at a day care; his wife described hearing shots whiz by as she chased the assailants. The most recent assassination was the Jan. 11, 2012 death of Mustafa Ahmadi-Roshan, an expert on uranium enrichment, also by a magnet bomb slapped on his car during his morning commute.

By then, Iran was trying to strike back. The task of avenging the scientists fell to the sprawling Quds Force's own covert-operations division, known as Unit 400. It took a shotgun approach, targeting Israeli diplomatic missions in a variety of countries, mostly in the developing world where the global antiterrorism mesh is not so fine. Exposed in Baku, Tbilisi, Johannesburg, Mombasa and Bangkok, the failures mounted at a pace that was itself one of the problems.

In the world of espionage, a quality covert operation can take years to pull together. Yet in the 15 months from May 2011 to July 2012, the Quds Force and Hizballah attempted 20 attacks, by the count of Matthew Levitt, a former State Department counterterrorism official. "Hizballah and the Quds Force traded speed for tradecraft and reaped what they sowed," Levitt writes in a January report for the Washington Institute for Near East Policy. "Quds Force planners were stretched thin by the rapid tempo of their new attack plan, and were forced to throw together random teams of operatives who had not trained together."

The decline in quality was so striking it initially inspired disbelief. Recall the preposterous-sounding plot weaving together a former used-car salesman, Mexico's Zetas drug gang and a bank transfer from a Revolutionary Guard account to assassinate Saudi Arabia's ambassador — by bombing a Washington restaurant? A year on it looks like the new normal.

In Bangkok, an Iranian agent entered a courtroom in a wheelchair, having accidentally blown his legs off while fleeing police. A January alert issued by Turkish intelligence was light on specifics but quite certain the Quds operatives would be staying in five-star hotels.

"There's a number of reasons that Iranian intelligence has suffered," says Meir Javedanfar, an Iranian-born analyst who lectures at the Interdisciplinary Center in Herzliya, Israel. "No. 1," he says, "is the 2009 uprisings in Iran." The street protests over a fraudulent election undermined the perceived legitimacy of the state among people who once would work for it, including in its secret services. "People less and less see it as a nationalist endeavor and more as a Khamenei-related project to strengthen himself," Javedanfar says, referring to Iran's Supreme Leader Ayatullah Ali Khamenei, who by some published accounts personally authorizes all overseas attacks.

Hard-liners further aggravated the situation by purging competent reformists from both the secret services and from Iran's embassies — crucial to a force expected to work undetected abroad. "Basically the Quds Force doesn't cooperate with the Foreign Ministry, and the Foreign Ministry isn't what it used to be either," says Javedanfar. Under President Mahmoud Ahmadinejad, 42% of ministry employees have only high school degrees. "The regime is a bigger threat to itself than Israel," he says.

Reva Bhalla, a senior analyst with Stratfor, the US private intelligence company with strong government security connections, said the strategy was to take out key people. "With co-operation from the United States, Israeli covert operations have focused both on eliminating key human assets involved in the nuclear programme and in sabotaging the Iranian nuclear supply chain," she said. "As US-Israeli relations are bound to come under strain over the Obama administration's outreach to Iran, and as the political atmosphere grows in complexity, an intensification of Israeli covert activity against Iran is likely to result."

"Israel has shown no hesitation in assassinating weapons scientists for hostile regimes in the past," said a European intelligence official, speaking on condition of anonymity. They did it with Iraq and they will do it with Iran when they can."

Mossad's covert operations cover a range of activities. Israeli and US intelligence co-operated with European companies working in Iran to obtain photographs and other confidential material about Iranian nuclear and missile sites. Israel has also used front companies to infiltrate the Iranian purchasing network that the clerical regime uses to circumvent United Nations sanctions and obtain so-called "dual use" items – metals, valves, electronics, machinery – for its nuclear programme.

The businesses initially supply Iran with legitimate material, winning Tehran's trust, and then start to deliver faulty or defective items that "poison" the country's atomic activities. "Without military strikes, there is still considerable scope for disrupting and damaging the Iranian programme and this has been done with some success," said Yossi Melman, a prominent Israeli journalist who covers security and intelligence issues for the Haaretz newspaper.

Mossad and Western intelligence operations have also infiltrated the Iranian nuclear programme and "bought" information from prominent atomic scientists. Israel has later selectively leaked some details to its allies, the media and United Nations atomic agency inspectors.

But Vince Canastraro, the former CIA counter-terrorism chief, expressed doubts about the efficacy of secret Israeli operations against Iran. "You cannot carry out foreign policy objectives via covert operations," he said. "You can't get rid of a couple of people and hope to affect Iran's nuclear capability."

The future of covert operations

A Time Magazine report revealed that Israeli intelligence services have scaled back their covert operations inside Iran. According to senior security officials who spoke to the magazine, operations have been reduced in areas such as high-profile missions, including assassinations and detonations at Iranian missile bases, as well as in recruiting spies inside the Iranian nuclear program, and efforts to gather on-the-ground intelligence.

The report further states that according to one official, the reductions have caused "increasing dissatisfaction" inside the Mossad, Israel's intelligence agency. Another official credits the reduced activities to the reluctance of Prime Minister Benjamin Netanyahu, who the official says is worried about the outcome of the operations being discovered.

Scaling back covert operations against Iran carries costs especially as Iran hurries to disperse its centrifuges into facilities deep underground. In one intelligence finding, an Israeli official says Iran itself estimates that sabotage to date has set back its centrifuge program by two full years. The computer virus known as Stuxnet is only the best known of a series of efforts to slow the Iranian program.

That effort involves a variety of governments besides Israel, involving equipment made to purposely malfunction after being tampered with before it physically entered Iran, says the report. The setbacks have prompted Iran to announce it would manufacture all components of its nuclear program itself — something outside experts are highly skeptical Tehran has the ability to actually do.

CIA Covert War

During both the Bush and Obama administrations, Iran and the United States have engaged in a shadow war that relies more on technology and human intelligence than conventional weaponry. Their covert campaigns include cyber attacks, espionage, and high-tech sabotage. Their common goal is to signal their resolve, impact each other's capabilities, and demonstrate the credibility of their deterrence – in turn swaying each other's decision-making.

The United States and Israel have reportedly worked together on a series of cyber attacks to slow or disrupt Iran's nuclear program since at least 2008. Although their origins are officially unknown, the Stuxnet worm reportedly attacked centrifuge production in late 2009 or early 2010, while the Flame virus collected information on Iranian officials in 2012.

The United States and Iran have used drones to gather intelligence and signal their offensive, defensive, and deterrent capabilities against each other. Drone technology has been an increasingly integral part of the United States intelligence and military arsenal over the past two decades. U.S. drones are far more advanced; they have been reportedly deployed in Afghanistan, Iraq, Libya, Pakistan and Yemen.

U.S. drone operations over Iran began after the start of the Afghanistan war; they reportedly increased after the 2003 invasion of Iraq. Specifics are classified but drones almost certainly monitored anti-American insurgent activity organized on Iranian territory. Over the last few years, drones may have spied on a wider array of Tehran's assets, including its nuclear program.

Iran's drone technology has also improved in recent years, possibly with help from Russia and China. Tehran unveiled the Karrar —its first home-made long-range drone—in August 2010. But experts have been skeptical about its capabilities and Iran's ability to guide the drone over long distances. In September 2012, the Revolutionary Guards unveiled the Shahed 129, an attack and surveillance drone with a purported range of up to 1,200 miles.

Tehran reportedly captured a U.S. RQ-170 Sentinel drone in late 2011 and subsequently claimed to have decoded its data and copied its technology. In late 2012, Iran claimed that it captured a U.S. ScanEagle drone, which the United States denied. But in December 2012, Secretary of Defense Leon E.

Panetta warned that the United States needs to keep track of the surveillance capability of Iran's drones.

Like many military platforms, drones can accomplish a variety of objectives. In October 2012, Israel shot down an Iranian drone reportedly near Dimona, where Israel's nuclear weapons program is believed to be based. The drone was reportedly launched by the Lebanese militia Hezbollah, which is supplied by Iran. The use of this drone may have been intended to gather intelligence and test Israeli defensive capabilities, but also to signal the potential for an Iranian strike on Dimona in retaliation for a future U.S. or Israeli attack on Iran.

Military activities always entail the risk of an unintentional escalation. Iranian fighter jets reportedly fired on a U.S. drone over the Persian Gulf on November 1, but they failed to hit it. While no escalation developed in this case, the increasing build-up of opposing forces in the Gulf has raised the risk of an entanglement. Escalation would be even more likely to occur if one side attacks a military objective in international waters.

Iran is a powerful regional player, but it is not a superpower with the global ambitions of the former Soviet Union. Iran's gross domestic product pales in comparison to some individual U.S. states. It has limited ability to project beyond its borders, other than through proxies such as Hezbollah and Hamas.

Tehran wants to impose costs on the United States and Israel for their covert programs and to block or dissuade their further moves against the Islamic Republic. Iran's actions also demonstrate its ability to fight back unconventionally tit-for-tat. Iran is also signaling to key players in the Gulf, notably Saudi Arabia and the United Arab Emirates, that their help in any attack on Iran could carry hidden or unanticipated costs. Iran's actions are also probably driven by domestic politics. The government would have risked a loss of credibility if it had not responded to cyber attacks and assassinations of scientists.

Covert campaigns are integral to both U.S. and Iranian efforts. But they almost certainly cannot achieve the long-term objectives of either country. U.S. covert action is unlikely to compel Iran to fulfill its international obligations on its nuclear program. Iranian covert action is also unlikely to undermine U.S. resolve either

The Cameraman

President Mahmoud Ahmadinejad's personal cameraman, Hassan Golkhanban, who defected from his UN entourage in New York, brought with him an intelligence treasure trove of up-to-date photographs and videos of top Iranian leaders visiting their most sensitive and secret nuclear and missile sites.

The cameraman, who is in his 40s, is staying at an undisclosed address, presumably a CIA safe house under close guard. He stayed behind when Ahmadinejad, after his UN speech, departed New York with his 140-strong entourage. For some years, Golkhanban worked not just as a news cameraman but personally recorded visits by the Iranian president and supreme leader Ayatollah Ali Khamenei of top-secret nuclear facilities and Revolutionary Guards installations.

When he left Tehran in the president's party, his luggage was not searched and so he was able to bring out two suitcases packed with precious film and deliver it safely into waiting hands in New York.

The Iranian cameraman has given US intelligence the most complete and updated footage it has ever obtained of the interiors of Iran's top secret military facilities and various nuclear installations, including some never revealed to nuclear watchdog inspectors. Among them are exclusive interior shots of the Natanz nuclear complex, the Fordo underground enrichment plant, the Parchin military complex and the small Amir-Abad research reactor in Tehran.

Some of the film depicts Revolutionary Guards and military industry chiefs explaining in detail to the president or supreme leader the working of secret equipment on view. Golkhanban recorded their voices.

Late September, he took the precaution of sending his wife and two children out of Iran on the pretext of a family visit to Turkey. They are most likely on their way to the United States by now.

From his years as a member of the loyal Bassij militia, the cameraman earned the complete trust of Iran's security services and was able to reach his professional pinnacle as personal photographer for the two most eminent figures in the country, Khamenei and Ahmadinejad, with the task of recording their most confidential pursuits.

This was his second visit to New York. The first time, a year ago, US intelligence was able to make contact and persuade him to defect with his stock of priceless photos and film.

The next day, Ahmadinejad and the 140-strong delegation departed from the posh Warwick Hotel in midtown. They split after members of his entourage loaded up shampoo, shoes, soap, vitamins and other items in short supply at home because of the economic sanctions the West has imposed on Iran to curb their nuclear ambitions.

According to the Jaras website, Mr Khanban was able to slip out of the Warwick Hotel an hour before the Iranian delegation was due to leave for the airport under the pretext of doing some last-minute shopping for his son. He never returned.

Mossad – Saudi Intel Partnership

Stratfor leaks

While publicly underplaying the significance of WikiLeaks activity in combating government secrecy, senior execs and analysts at private US intelligence firm Stratfor privately described WikiLeaks founder Julian Assange as a "terrorist" and "delusion nut" who "needs to be water-boarded" and made to "move from country to country" for the "next 25 years". The emails, part of over five million ones to be released, also suggest that senior Stratfor staff were apparently aware of secret charges reportedly by the US government to indict Assange and didn't mind using "trumped up" charges to lock up the whistle blower well before WikiLeaks had gone after Stratfor.

Most of the Stratfor email exchanges dealing with WikiLeaks and Assange are between mid-2010 to mid-2011. By 2010, WikiLeaks had already made a name for itself. It had published a number of ground-breaking documents dealing with a wide range of topics, including secret Guantanamo Bay procedures, the Climategate emails, the 2008 Peru oil scandal, the Milton report on toxic dumping in Africa, thousands of pager messages made during 9/11 and more. Despite all this, 2010 would be the year that truly elevated the organization, with release of the infamous "Collateral Murder" video, the Afghan War Diary, the Iraq War logs, and more than 250,000 US diplomatic cables.

According to the emails, Stratfor began to turn its eye to WikiLeaks in 2010, particularly in regards to the releases pertaining to the United States. Stratfor was well aware of the Cablegate scandal months before WikiLeaks officially announced the release in 22 November 2010. In an email dated 6 June 2010, Fred Burton, Stratfor's vice-president for counter-terrorism and corporate security and former special agent with the US Diplomatic Security Service, converses with Michael Psillico, a US state department official, over the arrest of Bradley Manning for his alleged role in providing material to WikiLeaks.

The emails, dated 2 May 2007, show discussions between Fred Burton, Stratfor's vice-president of counter-terrorism, and analysts in regards to the alleged secret Saudi-Israeli intelligence alliance. The email exchange also shows that Stratfor execs considered pursuing their own business relationship with the Saudi monarchy or, as Burton called them, "sleezy arsehole ragheads."

Cyprus

Burton forwarded a short message to the general analyst email list which recounted HUMINT (human intelligence) on the alleged secret deal. The source claimed that Mossad offered covert assistance to the Saudis with "intelligence collection and advice on Iran." The city of Nicosia in Cyprus was cited in the email "as a primary transit hub into Riyadh."

Additionally, the source advised Burton that the Saudis "are playing both sides of the fence — with the jihadists and the Israelis — for fear that the US does not have a handle on either." The source also claimed that "several enterprising Mossad officers, both past and present, are making a bundle selling the Saudis everything from security equipment, intelligence and consultation," a statement that implies an established security and business relationship between the Jewish state and the Saudi monarchy.

The message by Burton was additionally shared with another list that included Stratfor's president and Chief Financial Officer Don Kuykendall. Burton inquired, "Have we got the Saudi Foreign Ministry or intel[ligence] services as sub clients? If not, [I] suggest we send Mike Parks [Stratfor employee with a history of getting clients for Stratfor], who is good friends with Prince Bandar, to sign them up. $100,000 deal is nothing to these folks. I think Les Janka also has contacts with these sleezy arsehole ragheads (sic)."

The idea seemed to resonate well with other Stratfor senior staff, although there were concerns whether Stratfor's budget would cover an employee's trip to Riyadh in order to charm out a deal. The email thread ended with Burton, typically tasteless in his humor, asking, "Either we want these towel heads as a client o[r] not. I can also have anybody we send to Riyadh beheaded."

The year 2007 was the year when Saudi Arabia officially reaffirmed its support for the Arab Peace Initiative. Moreover, a New York Times report in August of that year stated that Saudi Arabia's foreign minister, Prince Saud al-Faisal, was keen to be involved in the ill-fated Annapolis peace conference due to occur in the fall. In turn, Israel signaled its 'openness' to the Saudi plan.

Stuxnet malware

Saudi Arabia and Israel's Mossad intelligence division are co-conspiring to produce a computer worm "more destructive" than the Stuxnet malware to sabotage Iran's nuclear program. Ex- Saudi spy chief Prince Bandar bin Sultan and director of Israel's Mossad intelligence agency Tamir Bardo sent their representatives to a meeting in Vienna on November 24, 2013 to increase the two sides' cooperation in intelligence and sabotage operations against Iran's nuclear program. One of the major methods discussed was "the production of a malware worse than...Stuxnet."

Stuxnet, a computer worm discovered in 2010, formed the basis of a cyberattack that sabotaged Iran's uranium enrichment program. Its complexity prompted researchers to claim that it could only have been developed by a nation state. It was generally believed to have been developed by the US and Israel, with former NSA contractor and whistleblower Edward Snowden only confirming their covert roles in an interview in July 2013.

The intention behind the development of the new malware would be to spy on and destroy the software structure of Iran's nuclear program. The two spy chiefs brought with them teams of Israeli and Saudi cyber specialists to discuss "the production of a malware worse than Stuxnet to spy on and destroy the software structure of Iran's nuclear program. The plan would need a great deal of time and funding, with a rough figure of US $1 million being given as an estimate. It was apparently welcomed by Saudi Arabia with open arms.

New meeting

Saudi ex-spy chief Bandar met with Mossad's Bardo in Jordan's Aqaba port city, inciting some concern from Saudi Arabia's Crown Prince Salman bin Abdulazi, who had advised against Bandar engaging in direct consultations, instead deeming 'clandestine' discussions with Israel over strategic Middle Eastern issues more appropriate.

A recent agreement between Iran and the Group 5+1 (the US, Russia, China, France and Britain plus Germany) unsettled Saudi officials, with Bandar having previously denounced the interim deal as the *"West's treachery."* Israeli Prime Minister Benjamin Netanyahu lambasted the agreement, which was reached on November 23, 2013 as *"a historic mistake."*

On November 17, 2013 *The Sunday Times* reported that the Israeli Mossad intelligence agency and Saudi officials were working together to develop a contingency plan should Iran's nuclear program not be adequately curtailed. Both governments reportedly expressed concern that negotiations could result in concessions being made to Iran.

Meeting in Tel Aviv

CIA chief John Brennan made a "secret" visit to Israel to discuss an emerging nuclear deal between Iran and world powers, Israel's leftist *Haaretz* newspaper reported.
The visit came as a June 30, 2015 deadline looms for a deal that would row back Iran's nuclear program in return for relief from sanctions, which Israel has long opposed, causing friction between Jerusalem and the White House.

Brennan met his counterpart, Mossad chief Tamir Pardo, and other intelligence officials, as well as Prime Minister Binyamin Netanyahu, *Haaretz* reported, citing "senior Israeli officials."They discussed the emerging Iran deal and Tehran's "subversive" activities around the Middle East.

The report surfaces after Brennan stressed on *CBS News* last week that there is a "very, very strong relationship between United States and Israel on the intelligence, security and military fronts."

"It's one of the great things, I think, about our system; there can be policy differences between our governments but the intelligence and security professionals know that we have an obligation to keep our countries safe and secure," he added.

"And so although there's been great debate about the Iranian nuclear negotiations that are ongoing," continued Brennan, "the CIA, NSA and other intelligence community entities are working very close with their Israeli as well as other counterparts."

Great Middle East Project

Longstanding neocon dreams to partition Iraq into three along ethnic and religious lines have been resurrected. White House officials now estimate that the fight against the region's 'Islamic State' will last years, and may outlive the Obama administration.

But this 'long war' vision goes back to nebulous ideas formally presented by late RAND Corp analyst Laurent Muraweic before the Pentagon's Defense Policy Board at the invitation of then chairman Richard Perle. That presentation described Iraq as a "tactical pivot" by which to transform the wider Middle East.

Brian Whitaker, former Guardian Middle East editor, rightly noted that the Perle-RAND strategy drew inspiration from a 1996 paper published by the Israeli Institute for Advanced Strategic and Political Studies, co-authored by Perle and other neocons who held top positions in the post-9/11 Bush administration.

The policy paper advocated a strategy that bears startling resemblance to the chaos unfolding in the wake of the expansion of the 'Islamic State' — Israel would "shape its strategic environment" by first securing the removal of Saddam Hussein. "Jordan and Turkey would form an axis along with Israel to weaken and 'roll back' Syria." This axis would attempt to weaken the influence of Lebanon, Syria and Iran by "weaning" off their Shi'ite populations. To succeed, Israel would need to engender US support, which would be obtained by Benjamin Netanyahu formulating the strategy "in language familiar to the Americans by tapping into themes of American administrations during the cold war."

The 2002 Perle-RAND plan was active in the Bush administration's strategic thinking on Iraq shortly before the 2003 war. According to US private intelligence firm Stratfor, in late 2002, then vice-president Dick Cheney and deputy defense secretary Paul Wolfowitz had co-authored a scheme under which central Sunni-majority Iraq would join with Jordan; the northern Kurdish regions would become an autonomous state; all becoming separate from the southern Shi'ite region.

The strategic advantages of an Iraq partition, Stratfor argued, focused on US control of oil:

The expansion of the 'Islamic State' has provided a pretext for the fundamental contours of this scenario to unfold, with the US and British looking to re-establish a long-term military presence in Iraq in the name of the "defense of a young new state."

In 2006, Cheney's successor, Joe Biden, also indicated his support for the 'soft partition' of Iraq along ethno-religious lines – a position which the co-author of the Biden-Iraq plan, Leslie Gelb of the Council on Foreign Relations, now argues is "the only solution" to the current crisis.

Also in 2006, the Armed Forces Journal published a map of the Middle East with its borders thoroughly re-drawn, courtesy of Lt. Col. (ret.) Ralph Peters, who had previously been assigned to the Office of the Deputy Chief of Staff for Intelligence where he was responsible for future warfare. As for the goals of this plan, apart from "security from terrorism" and "the prospect of democracy", Peters also mentioned "access to oil supplies in a region that is destined to fight itself."

In 2008, the strategy re-surfaced – once again via RAND Corp – through a report funded by the US Army Training and Doctrine Command on how to prosecute the 'long war.' Among its strategies, one scenario advocated by the report was 'Divide and Rule' which would involve:

The Sionist strategy

Almost thirty years ago, a prominent group of neoconservative hawks found an effective vehicle for advocating their views via the Committee on the Present Danger, a group that fervently believed the United States was a hair away from being militarily surpassed by the Soviet Union, and whose raison d'être was strident advocacy of bigger military budgets, near-fanatical opposition to any form of arms control and zealous championing of a Likudnik Israel. Considered a marginal group in its nascent days during the Carter Administration, with the election of Ronald Reagan in 1980 CPD went from the margins to the center of power.

Just as the right-wing defense intellectuals made CPD a cornerstone of a shadow defense establishment during the Carter Administration, so, too, did the right during the Clinton years, in part through two organizations: the Jewish Institute for National Security Affairs (JINSA) and the Center for Security Policy (CSP). And just as was the case two decades ago, dozens of their members have ascended to powerful government posts, where their advocacy in support of the same agenda continues, abetted by the out-of-government adjuncts from which they came.

Industrious and persistent, they've managed to weave a number of issues-- support for national missile defense, opposition to arms control treaties, championing of wasteful weapons systems, arms aid to Turkey and American unilateralism in general--into a hard line, with support for the Israeli right at its core.

On no issue is the JINSA/CSP hard line more evident than in its relentless campaign for war--not just with Iraq, but "total war," as Michael Ledeen, one of the most influential JINSAns in Washington, put it last year. For this crew, "regime change" by any means necessary in Iraq, Iran, Syria, Saudi Arabia and the Palestinian Authority is an urgent imperative. Anyone who dissents--be it Colin Powell's State Department, the CIA or career military officers--is committing heresy against articles of faith that effectively hold there is no difference between US and Israeli national security interests, and that the only way to assure continued safety and prosperity for both countries is through hegemony in the Middle East--a hegemony achieved with the traditional cold war recipe of feints, force, clientism and covert action.

For example, the Pentagon's Defense Policy Board--chaired by JINSA/CSP adviser and former Reagan Administration Defense Department official Richard Perle, and stacked with advisers from both groups--recently made news by listening to a briefing that cast Saudi Arabia as an enemy to be brought to heel through a number of potential mechanisms, many of which mirror JINSA's recommendations, and which reflect the JINSA/CSP crowd's preoccupation with Egypt. (The final slide of the Defense Policy Board presentation proposed that "Grand Strategy for the Middle East" should concentrate on "Iraq as the tactical pivot, Saudi Arabia as the strategic pivot [and] Egypt as the prize.")

Ledeen has been leading the charge for regime change in Iran, while old comrades like Andrew Marshall and Harold Rhode in the Pentagon's Office of Net Assessment actively tinker with ways to re-engineer both the Iranian and Saudi governments. JINSA is also cheering the US military on as it tries to secure basing rights in the strategic Red Sea country of Eritrea, happily failing to mention that the once-promising secular regime of President Isaiais

Afewerki continues to slide into the kind of repressive authoritarianism practiced by the "axis of evil" and its adjuncts.

Indeed, there are some in military and intelligence circles who have taken to using "axis of evil" in reference to JINSA and CSP, along with venerable repositories of hawkish thinking like the American Enterprise Institute and the Hudson Institute, as well as defense contractors, conservative foundations and public relations entities underwritten by far-right American Zionists (all of which help to underwrite JINSA and CSP).

It's a milieu where ideology and money seamlessly blend: "Whenever you see someone identified in print or on TV as being with the Center for Security Policy or JINSA championing a position on the grounds of ideology or principle--which they are unquestionably doing with conviction--you are, nonetheless, not informed that they're also providing a sort of cover for other ideologues who just happen to stand to profit from hewing to the Likudnik and Pax Americana lines," says a veteran intelligence officer.

JINSA / CSP

Founded in 1976 by neoconservatives concerned that the United States might not be able to provide Israel with adequate military supplies in the event of another Arab-Israeli war, over the past twenty-five years JINSA has gone from a loose-knit proto-group to a $1.4-million-a-year operation with a formidable array of Washington power players on its rolls.

Until the beginning of the previous Bush Administration, JINSA's board of advisers included such heavy hitters as Dick Cheney, John Bolton and Douglas Feith, the third-highest-ranking executive in the Pentagon during W. Bush administration. Both Perle and former Director of Central Intelligence James Woolsey, two of the loudest voices in the attack-Iraq chorus, are still on the board, as are such Reagan-era relics as Jeane Kirkpatrick, Eugene Rostow and Ledeen--Oliver North's Iran/*contra* liaison with the Israelis.

According to its website, JINSA exists to "educate the American public about the importance of an effective US defense capability so that our vital interests as Americans can be safeguarded" and to "inform the American defense and foreign affairs community about the important role Israel can and does play in bolstering democratic interests in the Mediterranean and the Middle East." In practice, this translates into its members producing a steady stream of op-eds and reports that have been good indicators of what the Pentagon's civilian leadership is thinking.

JINSA relishes denouncing virtually any type of contact between the US government and Syria and finding new ways to demonize the Palestinians. To give but one example (and one that kills two birds with one stone): According to JINSA, not only is Yasir Arafat in control of all violence in the occupied territories, but he orchestrates the violence solely "to protect Saddam.... Saddam is at the moment Arafat's only real financial supporter.... [Arafat] has no incentive to stop the violence against Israel and allow the West to turn its attention to his mentor and paymaster."

And if there's a way to advance other aspects of the far-right agenda by intertwining them with Israeli interests, JINSA doesn't hesitate there, either. A recent report contends that the Arctic National Wildlife Refuge must be tapped because "the Arab oil-producing states" are countries "with interests inimical to ours," but Israel "stand[s] with us when we need [Israel]," and a US policy of tapping oil under ANWR will "limit [the Arabs'] ability to do damage to either of us."

The bulk of JINSA's modest annual budget is spent on taking a bevy of retired US generals and admirals to Israel, where JINSA facilitates meetings between Israeli officials and the still-influential US flag officers, who, upon their return to the States, happily write op-eds and sign letters and advertisements championing the Likudnik line. (Sowing seeds for the future, JINSA also takes US service academy cadets to Israel each summer and sponsors a lecture series at the Army, Navy and Air Force academies.)

In one such statement, issued soon after the outbreak of the latest intifada, twenty-six JINSAns of retired flag rank, including many from the advisory board, struck a moralizing tone, characterizing Palestinian violence as a "perversion of military ethics" and holding that "America's role as facilitator in this process should never yield to America's responsibility as a friend to Israel," as "friends don't leave friends on the battlefield."

However high-minded this might sound, the post service associations of the letter's signatories--which are almost always left off the organization's website and communiqués--ought to require that the phrase be amended to say "friends don't leave friends on the battlefield, especially when there's business to be done and bucks to be made." Almost every retired officer who sits on

JINSA's board of advisers or has participated in its Israel trips or signed a JINSA letter works or has worked with military contractors who do business with the Pentagon and Israel.

While some keep a low profile as self-employed "consultants" and avoid mention of their clients, others are less shy about their associations, including with the private mercenary firm Military Professional Resources International, weapons broker and military consultancy Cypress International and SY Technology, whose main clients include the Pentagon's Missile Defense Agency, which oversees several ongoing joint projects with Israel.

Military-Industrial Complex

The behemoths of military contracting are also well represented in JINSA's ranks. For example, JINSA advisory board members Adm. Leon Edney, Adm. David Jeremiah and Lieut. Gen. Charles May, all retired, have served Northrop Grumman or its subsidiaries as either consultants or board members. Northrop Grumman has built ships for the Israeli Navy and sold F-16 avionics and E-2C Hawkeye planes to the Israeli Air Force (as well as the Longbow radar system to the Israeli army for use in its attack helicopters).

It also works with Tamam, a subsidiary of Israeli Aircraft Industries, to produce an unmanned aerial vehicle. Lockheed Martin has sold more than $2 billion worth of F-16s to Israel since 1999, as well as flight simulators, multiple-launch rocket systems and Seahawk heavyweight torpedoes. At one time or another, General May, retired Lieut. Gen. Paul Cerjan and retired Adm. Carlisle Trost have labored in LockMart's vineyards. Trost has also sat on the board of General Dynamics, whose Gulfstream subsidiary has a $206 million contract to supply planes to Israel to be used for "special electronics missions."

By far the most profitably diversified of the JINSAns is retired Adm. David Jeremiah. President and partner of Technology Strategies & Alliances Corporation (described as a "strategic advisory firm and investment banking firm engaged primarily in the aerospace, defense, telecommunications and electronics industries"), Jeremiah also sits on the boards of Northrop Grumman's Litton subsidiary and of defense giant Alliant Techsystems, which--in partnership with Israel's TAAS--does a brisk business in rubber bullets. And he had a seat on the Pentagon's Defense Policy Board, chaired by Perle.

About the only major defense contractor without a presence on JINSA's advisory board is Boeing, which has had a relationship with Israeli Aircraft Industries for thirty years. (Boeing also sells F-15s to Israel and, in partnership with Lockheed Martin, Apache attack helicopters, a ubiquitous weapon in the occupied territories.)

But take a look at JINSA's kindred spirit in things pro-Likud and pro-Star Wars, the Center for Security Policy, and there on its national security advisory council are Stanley Ebner, a former Boeing executive; Andrew Ellis, vice president for government relations; and Carl Smith, a former staff director of the Senate Armed Services Committee who, as a lawyer in private practice, has counted Boeing among his clients. "JINSA and CSP," says a veteran Pentagon analyst, "may as well be one and the same."

Not a hard sell: There's always been considerable overlap beween the JINSA and CSP rosters--JINSA advisers Jeane Kirkpatrick, Richard Perle and Phyllis Kaminsky also served on CSP's advisory council; current JINSA advisory board chairman David Steinmann sits on CSP's board of directors; and before returning to the Pentagon Douglas Feith served as the board's chair. At this writing, twenty-two CSP advisers--including additional Reagan-era remnants like Elliott Abrams, Ken deGraffenreid, Paula Dobriansky, Sven Kraemer, Robert Joseph, Robert Andrews and J.D. Crouch--have recoccupied key positions in the national security establishment, as have other true believers of more recent vintage.

While CSP boasts an impressive advisory list of hawkish luminaries, its star is Frank Gaffney, its founder, president and CEO. A protégé of Perle going back to their days as staffers for the late Senator Henry "Scoop" Jackson (*a k a* the Senator from Boeing, and the Senate's most zealous champion of Israel in his day), Gaffney later joined Perle at the Pentagon, only to be shown the door by Defense Secretary Frank Carlucci in 1987, not long after Perle left.

Gaffney then reconstituted the latest incarnation of the Committee on the Present Danger. Beyond compiling an A-list of influential conservative hawks, Gaffney has been prolific over the past fifteen years, churning out a constant stream of reports (as well as regular columns for the *Washington Times*) making the case that the gravest threats to US national security are China, Iraq, still-undeveloped ballistic missiles launched by rogue states, and the passage of or adherence to virtually any form of arms control treaty.

Gaffney and CSP's prescriptions for national security have been fairly simple: Gut all arms control treaties, push ahead with weapons systems virtually everyone agrees should be killed (such as the V-22 Osprey), give no quarter to the Palestinians and, most important, go full steam ahead on just about every national missile defense program. (CSP was heavily represented on the late-1990s Commission to Assess the Ballistic Missile Threat to the United States, which was instrumental in keeping the program alive during the Clinton years.)

Looking at the center's affiliates, it's not hard to see why: Not only are makers of the Osprey (Boeing) well represented on the CSP's board of advisers but so too is Lockheed Martin (by vice president for space and strategic missiles Charles Kupperman and director of defense systems Douglas Graham). Former TRW executive Amoretta Hoeber is also a CSP adviser, as is former Congressman and Raytheon lobbyist Robert Livingston. Ball Aerospace & Technologies--a major manufacturer of NASA and Pentagon satellites--is represented by former Navy Secretary John Lehman, while missile-defense computer systems maker Hewlett-Packard is represented by George Keyworth, who is on its board of directors. And the Congressional Missile Defense Caucus and Osprey (or "tilt rotor") caucus are represented by Representative Curt Weldon and Senator Jon Kyl.

CSP was instrumental in developing the arguments against the Anti-Ballistic Missile Treaty. Largely ignored or derided at the time, a 1995 CSP memo co-written by Douglas Feith holding that the United States should withdraw from the ABM treaty has essentially become policy, as have other CSP reports opposing the Comprehensive Test Ban Treaty, the Chemical Weapons Convention and the International Criminal Court.

A Clean Break

But perhaps the most insightful window on the JINSA/CSP policy worldview comes in the form of a paper Perle and Feith collaborated on in 1996 with six others under the auspices of the Institute for Advanced Strategic and Political Studies. Essentially an advice letter to ascendant Israeli politician Benjamin Netanyahu, "A Clean Break: A New Strategy for Securing the Realm" makes for insightful reading as a kind of US-Israeli neoconservative manifesto.

The paper's first prescription was for an Israeli rightward economic shift, with tax cuts and a selloff of public lands and enterprises--moves that would also engender support from a "broad bipartisan spectrum of key pro-Israeli

Congressional leaders." But beyond economics, the paper essentially reads like a blueprint for a mini-cold war in the Middle East, advocating the use of proxy armies for regime changes, destabilization and containment.

Indeed, it even goes so far as to articulate a way to advance right-wing Zionism by melding it with missile-defense advocacy. "Mr. Netanyahu can highlight his desire to cooperate more closely with the United States on anti-missile defense in order to remove the threat of blackmail which even a weak and distant army can pose to either state," it reads. "Not only would such cooperation on missile defense counter a tangible physical threat to Israel's survival, but it would broaden Israel's base of support among many in the United States Congress who may know little about Israel, but care very much about missile defense"-- something that has the added benefit of being "helpful in the effort to move the US embassy in Israel to Jerusalem."

Though the general agenda put forth by JINSA and CSP continues to be reflected in councils of war, even some of the hawks (including Rumsfeld deputy Paul Wolfowitz) are growing increasingly leery of Israel's settlements policy and Gaffney's relentless support for it. Indeed, his personal stock in Bush Administration circles is low. "Gaffney has worn out his welcome by being an overbearing gadfly rather than a serious contributor to policy," says a senior Pentagon political official. Since earlier this year, White House political adviser Karl Rove has been casting about for someone to start a new, more mainstream defense group that would counter the influence of CSP. According to those who have communicated with Rove on the matter, his quiet efforts are in response to complaints from many conservative activists who feel let down by Gaffney, or feel he's too hard on President Bush. "A lot of us have taken [Gaffney] at face value over the years," one influential conservative says. "Yet we now know he's pushed for some of the most flawed missile defense and conventional systems. He considered Cuba a 'classic asymmetric threat' but not Al Qaeda. And since 9/11, he's been less concerned with the threat to America than to Israel."

ISIS and Israel

Why is IS — formerly known as the Islamic State in Iraq and Syria (ISIS) — not fighting Israel? Would anything change if its fighters were to gain access to the borders with occupied Palestine?

While the Israeli military machine was massacring people in Gaza — and amid the euphoria among some jihadis over the news of the announcement of an "Islamic caliphate" — video footage of masked individuals firing rockets into Israel was posted online, and attributed to IS. Many cheered for what they saw as the "Muslim caliph's" response to calls for succor from the people of Gaza, even believing the "caliphate" was very close to liberating Jerusalem. But the euphoria did not last very long.

The video turned out to be from an old footage dating back to 2012, recorded by the militant group known as the Mujahideen Shura Council, and was repurposed to be attributed to IS. IS-affiliated social media activists such as Turujman al-Asawirti were also quick to question the authenticity of the video attributed to their group.

Al-Akhbar had a number of questions for IS supporters from Lebanon, Syria, and Iraq, including the following: Why has IS maintained its distance from the events in Palestine? Are the people of Gaza not Muslims after all? Does this posture not reinforce the premise that there is a hidden link between Zionism and Salafi-Jihadism that appeases Israel, or is geography alone to blame for their inaction?

In a speech by IS leader Abu Bakr al-Baghdadi, after he installed himself as caliph of the Muslims, he spoke about the terror inflicted on Palestine, but he did so only in passing, in the wider context of the terror Muslims face around the world.

In substance, they believe that liberating Palestine is irrelevant without the establishment of the caliphate in the countries surrounding Palestine first. Before him, in the time of the late leader of al-Qaeda Osama bin Laden, the jihadi attitude on Palestine was also controversial. Why have the jihadis never declared Palestine an arena for their jihad?

In effect, the leader of global jihadism Sheikh Ayman al-Zawahiri had an interesting position, approaching the issue from the angle of priorities on the basis of "Dar al-Kufr and Dar al-Islam," or the abode of disbelief and the abode of belief in jihadi lore. Zawahiri argues that fighting in Palestine should be on the basis that it is an abode of Islam, and that therefore, liberating it is a duty for every Muslim, as stated in his speech "truths about the conflict between Islam and infidelity" in 2007. But despite this, Palestine remains at the bottom of the list of priorities for most jihadis.

In form, most adherents of Salafi-Jihadism believe that "Shias are more dangerous than Jews." In substance, they believe that liberating Palestine is irrelevant without the establishment of the caliphate in the countries surrounding Palestine first.

Sources linked to IS told *Al-Akhbar*, "The final war that will liberate Palestine will be led by the caliphate, preceded by the establishment of this state in the Levant and Iraq," on the basis of sayings they attribute to Prophet Mohammad. The sources add, "Allah alone knows just how much the soldiers of the caliphate yearn for skipping the necessary stages and battle the Jews in Palestine, but he who rushes something before its time comes shall be punished by being denied it."

The sources, who are based in the Raqqa province of Syria, enumerate these necessary stages, saying, "The priority is to liberate Baghdad, then head to Damascus and liberate all of the Levant, before liberating Palestine."

This is the principle that IS soldiers follow: "Fighting nearby apostates is more important than fighting faraway infidels." To justify this, they rely on the Wars of Apostasy initiated by the Caliph Abu Bakr (against Muslims who renounced their religion following the death of the Prophet), who made it a priority over fighting infidels and Muslim conquests.

According to IS fighters, the adherents of all Islamic sects who do not submit to their "caliph" are either "apostates or misguided folk, who should be fought and killed, forced to repent and let themselves be guided, or be liberated from apostate rule." A jihadi adds here, "We the followers of this path follow sharia not the whims of men," adding that the Prophet had fought Quraysh first before moving on to fight the Jews of Banu Qurayza.

These sharia-based arguments are "reinforced" by the reality on the ground. A jihadi argues, "No one can initiate a battle against Israel except through the [direct] borders." The jihadi then adds sarcastically, "Certainly, the mujahideen will not be able to bomb Israel by air," before he said, "IS is still far from Israel. If it reaches Jordan and southern Syria (the Golan and Quneitra), then things would be different."

The jihadis base their vision on their perception that "Syria, Lebanon, Egypt, and Jordan all collaborate with Israel," and argue that any attack they initiate would be stopped by what they call the "idolatry" regimes in the name of security. A jihadi opines, "Since the countries adjacent to Israel do not fire a single bullet at it, this means they do not want a confrontation with Israel. Any attempt to use their territories to target Israel means automatically a confrontation with these regimes. Therefore, we must first purge these countries to get to Israel."

The IS-affiliated jihadis conclude that "the enmity the Arab countries and Arab groups have with Israel are in words not deeds, that is, only in politics and slogans. As long as this is the case, any group that wants to operate will confront these regimes." As proof of their point, the jihadis give the example of the Abdullah Azzam Brigades' operations out of South Lebanon, and the subsequent crackdown on the group's members after they fired rockets into Israel. For this reason, these jihadis believe that the priority is for their "state" to expand gradually, and that everything else is meaningless and illogical.

With regards to suicide operations, the jihadis said, "This is on the table, but the time for it has not yet come."

Mossad's chiefs about Iran

Meir Dagan

Former Mossad Chief Meir Dagan said that he would have resigned if Prime Minister Benjamin Netanyahu had decided to attack Iran's nuclear facilities. In his interview with Channel 10, Dagan said, "it was his fully within his authority to make such a decision, but I decided that I would resign at that moment."

In the interview, Dagan also showed the letter in which he requested to leave his post – responding to claims made by Netanyahu's associates that his criticism of the premier was due to personal reasons, after Netanyahu decided not to renew his tenure. "It hurts me that the prime minister is not telling the truth. This is simply not true. I can show you a letter I wrote to the prime minister, that I sent him, and I asked to end my term."

Dagan has granted several interviews over the last few weeks, criticizing Netanyahu's policies and behaviors, and headlined a left-wing rally in Tel Aviv, in which he said that Israel faces its worst crisis ever under Netanyahu's leadership.

Likud officials said of Dagan's speech that it was "strange that he now claims that he doesn't have faith in the current leadership, when he himself requested to extend his tenure as Mossad chief under the leadership of the prime minister.

In his resignation letter, presented on Channel 10, Dagan wrote: "*Sir, as you know, I conclude my tenure on 1/1/11. I recommend that a candidate be chosen in the near future to take on the task of Mossad chief, so that we can properly prepare him and ensure that his entrance into the position be as smooth as possible. If you would like to consult with me about a candidate, I am happy to do so. As such, I am concluding 42 years in the service of the state. I did the best that I could. I want to thank you for the faith and support that I received from you, and to thank Mr. Ariel Sharon who appointed me to the position, and Mr. Ehud Olmert, under whom I worked. I would also like to take this opportunity to wish you and your family and all of Israel and good and blessed year. Respectfully, Meir Dagan.*"

During the interview with Channel 10, Dagan also expressed his support for

Labor chief Isaac Herzog as prime minister: "In my eyes, he is not just a fitting candidate, but at this time, he seems to me to be the very best candidate to take on the role of prime minister."

Tamir Prado

Tamir Pardo, head of Mossad, had this to say to a roomful of Israeli ambassadors:

"What is the significance of the term existential threat?" the ambassadors quoted Pardo as asking. "Does Iran pose a threat to Israel? Absolutely. But if one said a nuclear bomb in Iranian hands was an existential threat, that would mean that we would have to close up shop and go home. That's not the situation. The term existential threat is used too freely."

Not only is Pardo going on the record to say that this language, favored by the very Prime Minister who appointed him to head Mossad, is overblown, but he did it in front of a roomful of Avigdor Lieberman's people. This takes guts: Defense Minister Ehud Barak recently found himself in trouble for going off message on Iran when he suggested that Israel is not the sole motive force behind Iran's nuclear talk.

Officially, Israel continues to criticize the talks and the pending nuclear agreement between the world powers and Iran. Prime Minister Benjamin Netanyahu and Defense Minister Moshe Ya'alon, each in his own way, keep bashing the negotiations.

It will take nearly three more months to flesh out the full details of a final and comprehensive agreement. President Obama says Iran's nuclear program will be reduced and rolled back so that it would take one year to "break out" to assemble a bomb. In return the West and the UN's sanctions will be gradually lifted.

Most Israeli experts, and certainly its leaders, have argued without hesitation that the current deal is dangerous to Israel's interests. But is it really? The blatant reality is that even before the deal Iran was already a nuclear threshold state. And if it really wants to, it can run off and produce nuclear weapons.

On the other hand, Israel is the strongest nation in the region. According to foreign reports, the only democracy in the Middle East boasts both a significant nuclear arsenal and submarines that are capable of executing second strikes — the capability to respond to a nuclear attack with powerful nuclear retaliation.

Four Arab states – Syria, Iraq, Libya and Yemen – are disintegrating. As a result, Israel's strategic posture has improved, as many of the serious military threats facing Israel have dissipated.

Israel would have preferred that there be no negotiations on Iran's nuclear ambitions, and that sanctions would be in place forever. But that won't happen. Without admitting it, Israel is preparing itself for the "day after," adjusting its position to the reality at the end of the negotiations.

The world will never hear an official admission, but deep in their heart Israeli leaders surely understand they failed to orchestrate an international campaign against the talks and the deal that has emerged.
It was an unnecessary campaign. Israel paid a heavy price in its confrontation with the US administration, and it caused great animosity between Netanyahu and President Barack Obama. Frankly, Israel had very little influence, if at all, on the talks.

The only tangible result was that Netanyahu won reelection last month, after convincing the public that only he knows how to deal with the threat of Iran becoming a nuclear state.
But now, with election season over and the deal with Iran being shaped, Israel has started clandestine diplomatic and intelligence initiatives to reach understandings and define red lines on how to deal with the upcoming reality.

Israeli bodies – the Defense Ministry, the air force, Military Intelligence and the Mossad – are already involved in discreet contacts with their American counterparts, as well as with EU countries, on how to prepare various responses in case Iran violates the deal.

The best-case scenario is that Iran will adhere to the agreement. But anyone who follows Iran's nuclear history and its relations with international bodies such as the International Atomic Energy Agency knows that it is unlikely to happen. Most probably Iran will try to dishonor its obligations through deceptions and lies.

Israel, with its counterparts, is trying to define the possible responses needed if and when Iran's deceptions are exposed. In the past, international media reported that Mossad chiefs met with their Saudi counterparts to coordinate joint efforts to stop Iran from building nuclear bombs. In these reports it said Saudi Arabia agreed that the Israel Air Force would use Saudi airspace for an attack on Iran's nuclear sites.

This doesn't mean that Israel is already coordinating a detailed military option with all those who are against the deal. These exchanges are more about reaching a basic understanding, should Iran seriously violate the deal.

Indeed, one should not hastily reach the conclusion that Israel is expediting its preparations to strike Iran. For now, Israel is still relying on the Americans. Ya'alon made it clear that Obama had promised that he would not allow Iran to have nuclear weapons.

But it is also clear that Israel will not tolerate a situation where Iran is on the verge of producing nuclear bombs. In such a worst-case scenario, it is most probable that any Israeli prime minister will make the same decision as previous leaders – Menachem Begin in 1981 and Ehud Olmert in 2007, who ordered to destroy Iraqi and Syrian nuclear reactors, respectively. Even though it's reported that Israel does have nuclear weapons it can't allow Iran, which advocates the destruction of the Jewish state, to have nuclear bombs.

Kill Mughniyeh

Imad Mughniyeh was born in 1962 in the Lebanese Shi'ite village of Tayr Dibba to a poor family of olive and lemon harvesters. He moved to Beirut as a child and despite his religious affiliation, he became active in the predominantly Sunni Palestinian al-Fatah movement.

In Lebanese Palestinian reports, Mughniyeh was even described as participating in the unit of bodyguards protecting then-PLO chief Yasser Arafat. But after the PLO chairman and his fighters were forced to leave Lebanon following the Israeli invasion in 1982 – just three years after the Islamic Revolution in Iran – Mughniyeh returned to his own religious cohort and joined Hezbollah, "The Party of God," a heavily armed Lebanese faction established and nurtured by Iran.

He quickly involved himself in some of the most outrageous Hezbollah attacks, proving his loyalty and his skills. He was trained by the chillingly skilled Iranian Revolutionary Guard Corps.

In a bloody two-year period – between November 1982 and September 1984 – he was a key player in several car bombing attacks against Israeli, American, and French targets in Lebanon. Among his trademarks: videotapes made by the suicide bombers and their accomplices nearby. The terrifying impact was thus magnified.

The attacks of those years included two assaults on Israeli military headquarters in the southern city of Tyre, which killed 150 Israelis and Lebanese.

He orchestrated the suicide bombings of the U.S. Marines barracks and a French military building in Beirut, killing 241 American servicemen, 58 French paratroopers, and six Lebanese civilians.

He was also a major actor in the bombing of the 1984 U.S. Embassy in Beirut, which killed 63 people. And this was just the beginning. His career would mushroom over the next two and a half decades.

In 1985, Mughniyeh personally participated in the hijacking of a TWA airliner. After it was forced to land in Beirut, a U.S. Navy diver among the passengers – Robert Stethem – was tortured and killed.

The first image of Mughniyeh, then just 22 years old, was first seen in the pages of the Western press when photographed waving his pistol near the TWA pilot's head in the cockpit. That photo was the key evidence used by U.S. law enforcement officials to indict Mughniyeh for murder in that incident. But for Israel, it would take another seven years to realize his significance.

The Hezbollah man was the architect of the 1992 bombing of the Israeli Embassy in Buenos Aires, Argentina, which killed 29 people – including seven Israelis, among them one Mossad agent. This was Mughniyeh's revenge for the Israeli helicopter attack that had killed Hezbollah's top leader, Abbas Moussawi.

The Buenos Aires attack led Israel to acknowledge two important facts: One, that Mughniyeh would avenge every Israeli attack on his organization; and two, that Mughniyeh had to be wiped out.

These realizations were further strengthened by an attack two years later, when along with his Iranian patrons, Mughniyeh masterminded the bombing of the Jewish community center in the Argentinian capital, which devastated the building and left 85 people dead.

From that point on, Israel used every opportunity it could to try to get rid of Mughniyeh. Numerous tentative plans were drawn up, but only three came into fruition.

In 1994, the Mossad conspired a devious plan to obliterate Mughniyeh: Lebanese agents working for the Mossad planted a car bomb aimed at Mughniyeh's brother Fuad. Anticipating that Mughniyeh would attend his brother's funeral, Israel planned to carry out their assassination of the Hezbollah military chief then: But Imad Mughniyeh, probably paranoid about possible attempts on his life, did not show up at the funeral.

A few months after Fuad's death, Israeli intelligence managed to obtain precise information that Imad Mughniyeh was scheduled to board a flight from Damascus to Tehran using a false name.

The Mossad informed the CIA of Mughniyeh's whereabouts, and the Americans orchestrated a redirection of the flight to Kuwait and dispatched a military plane from Saudi Arabia to bring Mughniyeh to justice in the U.S. courts.

But the CIA made a cardinal error: It disclosed to the Kuwaitis the identity of the wanted terrorist. Fearing retribution from Hezbollah should they accede to the U.S. demand, the Kuwaitis declined to order the passengers of the plane to disembark. Kuwait permitted the flight to take off to Tehran.

The next missed opportunity was completely the Israelis' fault. After the Israeli withdrawal from Lebanon in 2000, the senior echelon of Hezbollah – known as the top five – paraded along the Israeli border on a victorious patrol tour. Mughniyeh was among them.

Israeli reconnaissance photographed the five and transmitted the images to Aman (military intelligence) headquarters in Tel Aviv. They were identified; and an attack plan was put into motion. Drone aircraft that could fire missiles were launched.

Western intelligence sources say they were told by Israelis later that this was a "rare opportunity to disrupt Hezbollah's leadership." But the order to kill never came. Prime Minister Ehud Barak, who was proud of ordering the Israeli withdrawal from south Lebanon after 18 years of occupation, feared that the relative calm would be disrupted if he had Hebzollah's top leaders eliminated.

Senior officers in the Mossad were furious. Years of painstaking information-gathering efforts were wasted. But they had no choice but to accept their political leader's decision and to wait for the next opportunity.

Mughniyeh, as the years went by, became more cautious. Israeli intelligence learned that he went to a plastic surgeon in Beirut to alter his appearance.

He also moved to the safe haven of Tehran, where he enhanced his professional and personal ties with the Revolutionary Guards commanders – particularly with the charismatic General Qassem Soleimani, who was head of the elite Al-Quds force.

After returning to his Beirut headquarters, Mughniyeh continued to travel frequently among the triangle of the capitals of Lebanon, Syria and Iran.

The Mossad hunters, experts in human weaknesses and knowing that nobody is immune to error, waited patiently – but desperately.

Mughniyeh did indeed make mistakes, basically feeling too safe in the Syrian capital. He went to Damascus for both business and pleasure.

For his bloody business, he would meet with his master and friend, Iranian General Soleimani, to coordinate and plot strategy. Often joining them was General Muhammad Suleiman, top security adviser to Syrian President Bashar Assad and the man in charge of the regime's nuclear reactor and its special military ties with Iran and Hezbollah.

After working hours, Mughniyeh would enjoy the pleasures that Damascus had to offer: good food, alcohol and women – most of which he would not risk indulging in back home in the religious Shi'ite neighborhoods of Beirut.

Details of the "operation"

Piecing together human intelligence and telephone intercepts, Israeli intelligence managed to learn a great deal about Mughniyeh's private life and tracked his movements, finally aware of his post-plastic surgery appearance. They took advantage of two human weaknesses, quite uncharacteristic for a master terrorist on the run.

First, hosted by Syrian intelligence in one of its guest apartments, and in constant contact with Iranian "diplomats," Mughniyeh felt totally comfortable in Damascus. Living for decades with the assumption that he was an assassination target, he must have craved a place to feel safe. He let down his guard when in Syria, moving around with full self-confidence and no fear.

He also permitted himself to do, in Damascus, what he did not do at home in Lebanon: fool around with women. That, too, meant that he was literally a man about town, in moving cars more than a cautious man would be. Spies for the Mossad took note of routes that he repeatedly took.

Mughniyeh had an apartment in the posh neighborhood of Kafr Sousa, home to Syria's most wealthy businessmen and the military and intelligence cronies of the Assad regime. Feeling safe and secure due to his altered appearance and years of evading assassination attempts, Mughniyeh would travel in his SUV from Beirut to Damascus without bodyguards, often with his personal driver but sometimes alone.

Mughniyeh and other Hizbullah men lowered their guard and were relaxed while in Damascus, believing that they were beyond Israel's reach. Mughniyeh was walking alone, when a car bomb exploded.

The Mossad recruited a Syrian expat who visited his country often, and asked him to move to Damascus to provide logistics for the operation. The agent provided a villa to hide the vehicle and affix it with explosives, in addition to accommodations for the group that carried out the operation.

He rented the villa in an upscale suburb of Damascus ("Assad Villages"), located to the northwest of Kfar Sousa, and asked an ironsmith to separate the car entrance from the pedestrian entrance with an iron net on three sides, making it look like a cage and blocking the entry to the villa from that location.

A while later, the agent went back to Syria and bought a Mitsubishi Pajero 4×4, after knowing that several similar makes visited the targeted location often. In addition, Mughniyeh sometimes drove the same make. The execution team used a different model, Mitsubishi Lancer, due to its popularity in Syria in general.

The Pajero, now parked in the villa, was equipped with explosives in its trunk door. It was later discovered that, in addition to the explosives, the bomb contained metal pellets that can cause extensive damage to the target instantaneously. The device was similar to several bombs used by Israel to assassinate leaders in Lebanon and abroad.

The investigators and people close to the file are very secretive about the implementation team. But there are indicators that show that they were not Syrian citizens and that they had travelled in and out of the country to implement the operation.

In the early afternoon of 12 February 2008, one of the implementers drove the Pajero, equipped with explosives in its trunk door, and parked it outside the building frequented by Mughniyeh.

At dusk, the team of four individuals took the getaway Lancer and, after making sure that the construction workers had left the building under construction next to Mughniyeh's building, three of them went upstairs to observe the parking lot, the target, and the vehicle with the explosives.

They chose an apartment on the sixth floor. One of them surveyed the area with binoculars, another was charged with detonating the explosives, and the third was for protection. The fourth waited in the getaway car parked at the back of the building close to the fence.

Right before 10:20 pm, Mughniyeh exited the building and, as soon as he reached the well-lit lot nine meters away from the Pajero, the bomb was detonated and he was killed instantly.

Pe'al!" ordered the senior Mossad commander in charge of this extraordinary mission. Translated from Hebrew, this meant Go. Act. Push the button. The expert sitting beside the commander obeyed the order. He pushed the button. One hundred and thirty-five miles (215 km.) away in Syria's capital, Damascus, an explosion tore a notorious terrorist to bits.

The explosion was heard around 10:20 pm. Some people rushed to the location, including those Mughniyeh was seeing in the apartment. It turned out that when Mughniyeh had stepped out of the building's main gate, a 2006 silver Mitsubishi Pajero 4×4 parked nine meters away exploded, killing him alone, on the spot.

The implementing team left the building and headed toward their getaway car. They immediately drove toward the Mazzeh highway where they parked the car on the side of the road and left behind some items for distraction. The investigations showed that the implementing team faced a problem while escaping, which led them to leave the car and use another to escape to an unknown location.

This was a triumph for the men and women of Israeli intelligence. They had accomplished the nearly impossible. Their feeling was similar to the satisfaction Americans would enjoy, three years later, when Navy Seals found and killed Osama bin Laden.

A manhunt lasting a quarter of a century had come to an end. At Mossad headquarters at the Glilot Junction north of Tel Aviv there was great relief and even celebration.

In a most unusual example of operational cooperation, a CIA liaison officer was also in the Mossad HQ – part of the logistics and decision-making process for the assassination. The Israelis understood that officials at CIA headquarters in Langley, Virginia, were also very pleased.

Yet Israelis close to their country's intelligence agencies are telling Western officials something different: that the operation was almost entirely "blue and white" – referring to the colors of Israel's flag – with hardly any "red, white, and blue."

The Israelis were surprised to learn, during strategic talks with their counterparts in Washington, that the Americans were just as eager to get rid of him.

Since 1975, the CIA had been forbidden by Congress to carry out assassinations – even of America's worst enemies. But that policy changed after 9/11, when President George W. Bush ordered targeted killings using drone aircraft.

Nevertheless, in the eyes of the Bush administration – though not always understood by the Israelis – there was a huge difference between sending assassins and killing targets from the sky.

At a certain point during consultations with the Americans, then-Mossad director Meir Dagan proposed to his CIA counterpart, Gen. Michael Hayden, a joint operation to eliminate Mughniyeh.

Gen. Michael Hayden (as CIA director under President George W. Bush) agreed, but he set two conditions: First, that no innocent people would be hurt: The Americans were very concerned by the proximity of Mughniyeh's apartment to a girls' school; second, that only Mughniyeh would be targeted – and that none of his Syrian or Iranian acquaintances could be touched. The United States was reluctant to stir up violent conflicts with sovereign states.

At least according to what Israelis have been telling Western officials, the Mossad did not need the CIA for active management of the operation. They had already gleaned all the details necessary about Mughniyeh's daily routine and his hideout in Damascus.

The CIA was there, as they put it, to fill in any missing intelligence information and provide extra eyes in Damascus.

The Mossad certainly had its own excellent expertise, in its Kidon (Bayonet) special operations unit, when it came to killing terrorists. Still, the Israelis felt more comfortable having the CIA take part – even if the American role was seen as minor.

As agreed by Dagan and Hayden, a senior CIA official from its operations directorate was assigned to the Mossad team working on the project. The command center was in Tel Aviv.

Kidon operatives, along with Aman signals intelligence Unit 8200, monitored Mughniyeh almost around the clock, zooming in on his safe-house and the parking lot nearby. Based on previous operations, it can be assumed that the team had some physical presence in the area. It was decided that the weapon of choice would be a bomb planted in or on a car parked near Mughniyeh's apartment.

The CIA-Mossad relations hit a bump, for a while, when the Americans got cold feet and pulled out of the operation. The CIA began to reiterate its fears of the collateral damage that such an assassination would cause – concerned, despite Israel's assurances, about the girls' school nearby.

The Mossad was sorry to see the CIA pull out, but the preparations continued. Nevertheless, then-Prime Minister Ehud Olmert ordered the Mossad to make sure that the "killing zone" of the bomb be very narrow, so that only Mughniyeh would be touched.

The "toy factory" of the Mossad and the Aman agency – their technological units – began designing, assembling and testing the bomb. It was a laborious procedure, requiring dozens of tests, until the results were satisfactory and matched the guidelines stipulated by Olmert. The process was filmed, time and again, for analysis and dissection.

Contrary to the recent reports in the American media, the process of developing the bomb was carried out in Israel. Not in the U.S. Once Olmert was confident that the bomb would be highly accurate, officials say they have learned from Israel that Olmert brought the video clips to Washington. He showed them to President Bush and asked him to bring the CIA back into the operation. The video clearly showed that the diameter of the "killing zone" was no more than 10 meters. Bush was impressed. The next day, while he was still in the U.S., Olmert received a call from Dagan informing him that the CIA was back in.

The bomb was smuggled to Syria via Jordan, whose intelligence ties with the CIA and the Mossad had been tight and intimate for decades. The involvement of the CIA gave the Jordanians a sense of security in cooperating, in case of Hezbollah retribution.

There were two main obstacles to executing the operation. Mughniyeh's visits to his Damascus apartment were random and could not be predetermined by the surveillance teams. Secondly, it was difficult for the teams to ensure that they would be able to secure a spot for their rigged car to be parked near Mughniyeh or his vehicle.

Eventually, the conspirators found an undisclosed operational solution which would give them enough warning time ahead of Mughniyeh's arrival to prepare the trap.

The day of the assassination arrived: On the evening of February 12, Mughniyeh's car was spotted pulling into the parking lot. The Mossad planners breathed a sigh of relief. The school nearby was closed for the night. Even if the bomb was unexpectedly flawed, the innocent school girls were not at risk.

But to the agony of the project managers, when the car doors opened, Mughniyeh was not alone: Iranian commander Soleimani and the Syrian nuclear coordinator Suleiman exited the vehicle with him. At the command center in Tel Aviv, the order was given: Hold.

The three buddies went up to the apartment. In Tel Aviv, the Mossad project managers and their CIA liaison waited, nervously biting their nails, on the verge of losing hope. A few hours later, the information arrived that Soleimani and Suleiman had left the apartment and been picked up by a car. The planners could now only pray that Mughniyeh would not remain in the apartment overnight.

About half an hour later, the surveillance team reported that Mughniyeh had entered the parking lot and approached his car.
In Tel Aviv, the order rang out: *"Pe'al!"*

The master terrorist, the Hezbollah commander whose trademark was car bombing, fell victim to his own craft in a blast of poetic justice.

Kill Olmert

Mughniyeh's successor, Mustafa Badr Adin, ordered attacks on Israeli embassies and tried to assassinate Olmert and senior Israeli military officers and officials.

But Badr Adin repeatedly failed. His only success was in 2012 at Burgas airport in Bulgaria, when a Hezbollah suicide bomber killed five Israeli tourists and their Bulgarian driver.

Security precautions around Olmert were stepped up last year out of concern that Hezbollah would attempt to get at him. Olmert was in office not only at the time of the Mughniyeh killing but during the month-long war between Israel and Hezbollah in 2006.

Olmert, who is now facing additional corruption charges after being indicted in an Israeli court, is loathed by the majority of Israelis. But analysts who watch the country's security and defense policies believe that in those areas he was far-sighted, showed determination, and was willing to take risks.

In September 2007, just five months before ordering the assassination of Mughniyeh, Olmert unleashed Israel's covert operatives and then the air force to destroy the Syrian nuclear reactor that North Korea had helped build in a remote area.

One can only imagine what the world would look like had the reactor been built and operated in an area now controlled by the brutal Islamic State.

Six months after Mughniyeh's assassination, Olmert approved a covert operation in which Israeli long-range snipers – apparently firing from a ship – assassinated Syria's nuclear coordinator, Gen. Suleiman, while he dined with guests on the balcony of his villa overlooking the Mediterranean.

Days after Mughniyeh was killed, then Vice President Dick Cheney called Olmert and they exchanged congratulations for the successful operation. President Bush, too, held Olmert in high respect – reportedly telling someone he liked the Israeli leaders because "he has balls."

The man of Mossad

The alleged Israeli spy who reportedly infiltrated Hezbollah and frustrated attacks against Israel held a number of important positions, including supervising the personal security of the organization's leader, Hassan Nasrallah.

The alleged Mossad member was reportedly arrested weeks ago and held the position of deputy chief of Unit 910, which carries out operations against specific Israeli targets.

Mohammed Shawraba was a resident of a village in south Lebanon and comes from a family that includes religious figures known for their loyalty to Hezbollah. But sources added that Mohammed Shawraba arrest would not hurt his family, which "cannot be blamed for his deeds."

He reportedly advanced in Hezbollah until he became responsible for Nasrallah's personal security with an emphasis on surveillance.

After the spy was discovered, Hezbollah was quick to discharge the unit's fighters and spread them around to other units. The commander was similarly discharged after the spy reported his activities to US and Israeli intelligence.

The espionage involved more than one person – a cell – that was "the most serious [intelligence] breach in Hezbollah's history." Under questioning, it was revealed that Mossad made periodic payments totaling $1 million. Mossad spy worked undercover as a businessman and traveled a great deal.

Mossad allegedly recruited Mohammed Shawraba in a western Asian country. He worked with Mossad for a number of years and foiled many Hezbollah operations that were meant to avenge the assassination of commander Imad Mughniyeh in Damascus in 2008.

The double agent also supposedly exposed information about operatives operating abroad, leading to the arrest of Hezbollah agent Muhammad Amadar in Lima, Peru, in October.

The recurring failures of Unit 910 "caused a state of frustration in the party's ranks," and led to the creation of a separate secret unit run by Iran's Revolutionary Guards.

After close monitoring of the most important security officials, the unit arrested five Hezbollah members including the [Unit 910 deputy chief]. Hezbollah refuses to deny or confirm reports that Shawraba fed the Mossad intelligence on the Lebanese group's foreign-operations unit, which he had headed since 2008.

He was arrested with four people who worked for him in the group's foreign-operations unit, which works against Israeli interests in foreign countries, the newspaper reported. It said Hezbollah had become suspicious of Shawraba after five attempted retaliations against Israel over the Mughniyeh killing had failed.

Counter Espionage

On Jan. 5 2015, Hezbollah's deputy chief Naim Qassem lauded the ability of a group as "big and sophisticated" as Hezbollah "to stand with the same steadfastness despite some major infiltrations." Media outlets identified the latest accused spy as Mohammad Shorbah, but as Qassem implied, this was not the first such "major infiltration," nor is it likely to be the last.

But Israel doesn't always come out on top in this intelligence war. Hezbollah is no slouch when it comes to espionage and counter-intelligence, the result of training its operatives receive from Iran's Ministry of Intelligence and Security, and Hezbollah has enjoyed its share of successes against Israeli and Western security agencies.

In late 2000, a retired Israeli colonel named Elhanan Tannenbaum established a shady business relationship with Qais Obeid, a Palestinian criminal with ties to Hezbollah. Tannenbaum was lured first to Brussels, then the United Arab Emirates, where he was kidnapped and smuggled to Lebanon.
"I inform you gladly," Hezbollah leader Hassan Nasrallah announced at a Beirut conference, that Hezbollah now held an Israeli Army officer with ties to Israeli security agencies who was captured "in a new qualitative achievement and in a complicated security operation." Tannenbaum's kidnapping was an intelligence bonanza for Hezbollah. After three years, Tannenbaum and the bodies of the three soldiers were exchanged for 435 prisoners in Israeli jails.

In fact, Hezbollah's intelligence prowess dates back much earlier, and has targeted not only Israeli but also American intelligence services. In the mid-1990s, U.S. authorities investigating a local Hezbollah cell in New York quietly flew to South America on a lead. As soon as they landed they were paged by the New York field office. Photographs of the agents disembarking had just arrived on the office's fax machine in New York. More recently, in June of 2011, Nasrallah claimed that Hezbollah had identified at least two CIA spies within the group's ranks. "No one underestimates [Hezbollah's] capabilities," said one U.S. official at the time.

Nevertheless, the litany of failed Hezbollah operations over the past few years suggests Hezbollah's covert operational prowess has diminished. Public slip-ups included plots in Azerbaijan, India, Thailand and Egypt. Hezbollah agents were picked up by local authorities in Azerbaijan, Cyprus, Nigeria and Thailand and are now convicted felons serving jail time. More Hezbollah plots were thwarted this past year in Thailand and Peru — to cite just some of the recently foiled Hezbollah operations. Hezbollah's only success was the 2012 bombing of a tour bus in Burgas, Bulgaria.

Mughniyeh Sr. was killed in 2008, and Mughniyeh Jr. in 2015; Shorbah was arrested in 2014. Individual battles are won and lost, but the spy-vs-spy intelligence war between Hezbollah and Israel continues. Both sides see themselves as battling for survival, which means the espionage war is likely to continue at full force. In the words of espionage novelist John Le Carre, "Survival ... is an infinite capacity for suspicion" — and there's no shortage of suspicion between Israel and Hezbollah.

Seyyed Ahmed Dabiri

Highly credible Iranian exile sources in Europe have revealed that the Director of the Israel Desk of the Revolutionary Guards clandestine service was executed by a firing squad in late June or early July after he was accused of spying for Israel.

Aged 46, Seyyed Ahmed Dabiri was his codename. His real name is not known. The sources report that he was tried by a Guards martial court and found guilty of tipping Israel off on classified information, including the movements of Iranian military commanders in Syria, Iranian arms shipments to Syria and arms convoys bound for Hizballah in Lebanon.

Suspicion first fell on Dabiri after the Israeli air force struck the convoy of Iranian and Hizballah commanders that was on a top-secret visit to the village of Mazraat Amal near the Golan town of Quneitra on Jan. 18. They were there to survey the terrain preparatory to planting a Hizballah rocket position just across from IDF's Golan outposts, a mission which ended in disaster.

Killed in the attack were the Iranian general in charge of the Syrian front, Gen. Mohammad Ali Allah-Dadi, the high-ranking Hizballah intelligence officer Ali al-Tabtababni, who was in charge of liaison with the Iranian Guards, and Jihad Mughniyeh, son of the iconic Hizballah commander in chief, the late Imad Mughniye. He had been assigned command of the Hizballah Golan base whence to launch a new offensive against Israel.

After the air strike, the plan was abandoned, a setback with devastating effect on the Iranian and Hizballah high commands. Hizballah chief Hassan Nasrallah announced at the time that the gloves was now off against Israel and that "rules of engagement" with the Jewish state were no longer in force. No more than a handful of big shots were privy to the Golan tour in the highest Revolutionary Guards highest echelon and the inner circle of Nasrallah.

The IRGC's chief Gen. Ali Jafari and Iran's Middle East commander in chief Gen. Qassem Suleimani ordered an all-encompassing investigation to find out who was responsible for leaking to Israeli intelligence the secret of the Golan tour. According to the Iranian exiles, the high Hizballah command and the Guards headquarters in Tehran were exhaustively investigated.

DEBKA*file*'s sources point to the fact that on Jan. 5, two weeks before Israel's deadly air strike, Nasrallah's deputy, Sheikh Naim Qassem, complained that "Hizballah is battling espionage within its ranks and has uncovered some major infiltrations."

A short time earlier, in December 2014, Mohammad Shawraba, 42, the deputy chief of Unit 910, which is responsible for external terrorist operations, was arrested on suspicion of spying for Israel.

So in the weeks leading up to the Israeli Golan attack, Hizballah was buzzing with Israeli spy fever.Yet the Guards probe failed to discover the source of the leak either in Beirut or Tehran.When no Israeli mole was identified, the Guards intelligence chief Gen. Hassan Taeb set a trap and baited it with a false piece of intelligence.

On April 25, Israel air planes struck what they believed to be Syrian and Hizballah bases and arms dumps in the Qalamoun Mountains on the Syrian-Lebanese border. Middle East media carried confused reports on this attack — some claiming it targeted an arms convoy heading into Lebanon from Syria; others cited missile stores or even the Syrian army's 155th and 65th Brigades. Israeli sources declined to confirm or deny any of those versions.
The cause of the mix-up was that the target was a red herring. But the attack enabled Iranian spy catchers to narrow down the source and discover that Ahmad Dabiri was the mole who had tipped Israel off..

CHAPTER TWO

Destroying Tel Aviv

A senior figure in Iran's Revolutionary Guard Corps warned that should Israel launch an attack on his country, Tel Aviv would be destroyed instantly. *"If the Zionists were certain that they could win a war against us, they'd have initiated one by now, but since they don't have the strength to do so, they do nothing but threaten,"* said Mojtaba Zolnour, who represents Supreme Leader Ayatollah Ali Khamenei in the IRGC.

Should Israel nevertheless decide to strike Iran, the Islamic Republic's missiles will fall in the heart of Tel Aviv, *"even before the Zionists' missiles will reach us,"* he claimed, according to Iranian media. Zolnour's comments were reportedly a response to Foreign Minister Avigdor Liberman, that Israel was doing too much talking about Iran's alleged nuclear weapons program, and that *"if you want to shoot, shoot, don't talk."*

In an implied attack on Prime Minister Benjamin Netanyahu, the Yisrael Beytenu party chief recalled that when prime minister Menachem Begin decided to blow up Saddam Hussein's nuclear reactor at Osirak in 1981, *"we woke up the next morning"* to hear about it for the first time.

Similarly, in 2007, when Israel allegedly destroyed a Syrian nuclear reactor, *"there was no talk about it"* ahead of time, he said in an interview with Channel 2 news. Netanyahu has long threatened to attack Iran in order to destroy, or at least hobble, its nuclear program, although such threats have largely tapered off since the West launched nuclear negotiations with Tehran.

Another senior Iranian military official warned that any Israeli attack would unleash a firestorm of missiles on its cities fired by the Islamic Republic's Hezbollah allies in Lebanon.

The Shiite militia has more than 80,000 rockets ready to fire at Tel Aviv and Haifa, said General Yahya Rahim Safavi, military adviser to Iran's supreme leader Ayatollah Ali Khamenei. *"Iran, with the help of Hezbollah and its friends, is capable of destroying Tel Aviv and Haifa in case of military aggression on the part of the Zionists,"* he said, quoted on state television.

"I don't think the Zionists would be so unintelligent as to create a military problem with Iran," the general said. *"They know the strength of Iran and Hezbollah."* Israeli military officials meanwhile have tacitly conveyed a threat to the Lebanese group through international media.

New York Times reported, based on maps and aerial photography from IDF officials, that Hezbollah has moved most of its military infrastructure into and around the Shiite villages of southern Lebanon. According to the paper, Israeli officials say Hezbollah's move is tantamount to using the civilians as human shields.

The paper quotes Israeli officials saying the IDF will not be deterred from striking at Hezbollah posts, indicating that the villages would be hit even harder than during the 2006 Second Lebanon War. Hezbollah, meanwhile, is also mired in fights with rebels of nearly every Sunni group opposing Syrian President Bashar Assad, from Islamic State to the relatively moderate militias seeking to remove Assad from power.

A senior IDF intelligence official warned of a heightened threat of conflict over the next two years as a result of "escalation" in the region. In a briefing at the Defense Ministry in Tel Aviv, the official referred specifically to Hezbollah, and to Iran's arming of the group. Israel has repeatedly complained to the UN about Hezbollah's violations of UN Resolution 1701 from 2006, which forbids the group from rearming.

"The Iranian threat is a tangible threat to Israel," said the official, whose country has not ruled out the use of military force to block any attempt by Tehran to produce a nuclear bomb

Revolutionary Guards Corps

The IRGC is generally loyal to Iran's political hardliners and is clearly more politically influential than is Iran's regular military, which is numerically larger, but was held over from the Shah's era. The IRGC's political influence has grown sharply as the regime has relied on it to suppress dissent. Founded by a decree from Ayatollah Khomeini shortly after the victory of the 1978-1979 Islamic Revolution, Iran's Islamic Revolutionary Guards Corps (IRGC) has evolved well beyond its original foundations as an ideological guard for the nascent revolutionary regime ... The IRGC's presence is particularly powerful in Iran's highly factionalized political system, in which many senior figures hail from the ranks of the IRGC.

Through its Qods Force (QF), the IRGC has a foreign policy role in exerting influence throughout the region by supporting pro-Iranian movements and leaders. The QF numbers approximately 10,000-15,000 personnel who provide advice, support, and arrange weapons deliveries to pro-Iranian factions or leaders in Lebanon, Iraq, Syria, Persian Gulf states, Gaza/West Bank, Afghanistan, and Central Asia.

IRGC leaders have confirmed the QF is in Syria to assist the regime of Bashar al-Assad against an armed uprising, and it reportedly provided advisers to help the Iraqi government counter an offensive by the Islamic State (also known as ISIS or ISIL) that started in June 2014. The QF commander, Brigadier General Qassem Soleimani reportedly has a direct and independent channel to Khamene'i.

The QF commander during 1988-1995 was Brigadier General Ahmad Vahidi, who served as Defense minister during 2009-2013. He led the QF when it allegedly assisted Lebanese Hezbollah carry out two bombings of Israeli and Jewish targets in Buenos Aires (1992 and 1994) and is wanted by Interpol for a role in the 1994 bombing there. He allegedly recruited Saudi Hezbollah activists later accused of the June 1996 Khobar Towers bombing.

IRGC leadership developments are significant because of the political influence of the IRGC. Mohammad Ali Jafari has been Commander in Chief of the IRGC since September 2007. He is considered a hardliner against political dissent and a close ally of the Supreme Leader. He criticized Rouhani for accepting a phone call from President Obama on September 27, 2013, and has continued to oppose major concessions as part of a permanent nuclear settlement.

The *Basij militia* reports to the IRGC commander in chief; its leader is Brigadier General Mohammad Reza Naqdi. It operates from thousands of positions in Iran's institutions. Command reshuffles in July 2008 integrated the Basij more closely with provincially based IRGC units and increased the Basij role in internal security. In November 2009, the regime gave the IRGC's intelligence units greater authority, perhaps surpassing those of the Ministry of Intelligence, in monitoring dissent.

The IRGC Navy has responsibility to patrol the Strait of Hormuz and the regular Navy has responsibility for the broader Arabian Sea and Gulf of Oman (deeper waters further off the coast). As noted, the IRGC is also increasingly involved in Iran's economy, acting through a network of contracting businesses it has set up, most notably Ghorb (also called Khatem ol-Anbiya, Persian for "Seal of the Prophet"). Active duty IRGC senior commanders reportedly serve on Ghorb's board of directors and its chief executive, Rostam Ghasemi, served as Oil Minister during 2011-2013. In September 2009, the Guard bought a 50% stake in Iran Telecommunication Company at a cost of $7.8 billion.

The Wall Street Journal reported on May 27, 2014, that Khatam ol-Anbia has $50 billion in contracts with the Iranian government, including in the energy sector but also in port and highway construction. It has as many as 40,000 employees.

Back in 1979

Iran's Revolutionary Guard Corps (IRGC) was founded in the aftermath of the 1979 Islamic Revolution as an ideological custodian charged with defending the Islamic Republic against internal and external threats, but analysts say it has expanded far beyond its original mandate. Today, the IRGC presides over a vast power structure with influence over almost every aspect of Iranian life. Still, some experts say that while the corps is generally loyal to hard-line elements in the regime, it is far from a cohesive unit of like-minded conservatives.

The country's premier security institution of more than one hundred thousand strong, the IRGC fields an army, navy, and air force, while managing Iran's ballistic missile arsenal and irregular warfare operations through its elite Quds Force and proxies such as Hezbollah. It is also one of Iran's most influential economic players, wielding control over strategic industries, commercial services, and black-market enterprises. At the same time, the IRGC often serves as an incubator for senior Iranian public officials, making it especially powerful in the political sphere.

The Islamic Revolutionary Guard Corps was formed by late supreme leader Ayatollah Ruhollah Khomeini in the wake of the 1979 Islamic Revolution that ousted Shah Reza Pahlavi. The IRGC was originally created as a "people's army" similar to the U.S. National Guard; commanders report directly to the supreme leader, Iran's top decision-maker. Iran's president has little influence on their day-to-day operations.

Revolutionary Guards were created as a counterweight to the regular military, and to protect the revolution against a possible coup. In establishing the Guards, Khomeini was seeking to avoid a repeat of a successful 1953 coup that ousted a previous revolutionary government. But the Guards' activities in recent years have been aimed at protecting Iranian interests far beyond Tehran.

Current forces consist of naval, air, and ground components, and total roughly 150,000 fighters. The corps' primary role is internal security, but experts say the force can assist Iran's regular army, which has about 350,000 soldiers, with external defenses. Border skirmishes during the Iran-Iraq War in the 1980s helped transform the Guards into a conventional fighting force organized in a command structure similar to Western armies. The Guards also control Iran's Basij Resistance Force, an all-volunteer paramilitary wing, which, consists of as many as one million conscripts.

International Activities

The Guards began deploying fighters abroad during the Iran-Iraq War (1980-1988), "*exporting the ideals of the revolution throughout the Middle East.*" The Quds Force, a paramilitary arm of the Revolutionary Guard with 10,000 to 15,000 personnel, emerged as the de facto external affairs branch during the corps' expansion. Its mandate was to conduct foreign policy missions— beginning in Iraq's Kurdish region—and forge relationships with Shiite and Kurdish groups. The Quds Force has since supported and armed pro-Iranian militant groups across the Middle East and beyond, including in Lebanon, the

Palestinian territories, Iraq, Afghanistan, the Gulf states, and several others, according to the U.S. State Department.

The Guards' alleged involvement in Iraq was a particular point of contention between Washington and Tehran. Former president George W. Bush accused Iran in 2007 of providing roadside bombs to networks inside Iraq. That same year, coalition forces captured several militants in Iraq with alleged links to the Quds Force and Hezbollah. In October 2007, the U.S. Treasury Department designated the Quds Force a terrorist supporter for aiding the Taliban and other terrorist organizations.

In the wake of antigovernment protests throughout the Middle East in 2011, the United States and European Union have accused the Quds Force of providing weapons and other material support to help President Bashar al-Assad suppress the uprising in Syria. In October 2012, a member of the Quds Force pleaded guilty to plotting the assassination of the Saudi ambassador to the United States.

Player at Home

The alleged spread of the Revolutionary Guards' external influence coincides with a growing cachet at home. The Revolutionary Guards are the spine of the current political structure in Iran and a major player in the Iranian economy. The Guards' political influence began its ascendancy as a counterweight to former reformist president Mohammad Khatami. But the number of former Guards entering political life spiked during President Mahmoud Ahmadinejad's first term, beginning in 2005.

Supreme Leader Ali Khamenei has appointed former Revolutionary Guards commanders to top political posts like the presidency (Ahmadinejad) and major institutions, like the Islamic Republic of Iran Broadcasting Corporation (Ezzatollah Zarghami), the Supreme National Security Council (Saeed Jalili), and the Expediency Council (Mohsen Rezaei, a 2009 presidential challenger).

Amid deepening discord between Khamenei and Ahmadinejad in 2011, the IRGC began to target some of the president's allies. The IRGC benefits from the confrontation between Khamenei and Ahmadinejad because it makes Khamenei more dependent on the power and muscle of the IRGC.

Basij Force

Much of the institution's rise to prominence over competing militias and paramilitaries in the post-revolutionary period was due to its effectiveness in suppressing internal dissent. Guardsmen and Basij volunteers have a history of violently crushing riots in Iranian cities, and a unit dedicated to quelling civil unrest, the Ashura Brigades, was established in 1993.

In 2007, the Basij was brought under direct command of the Revolutionary Guards by Major General Mohammad Ali Jafari. The move officially refocused the organization on defending against the type of non-violent "velvet revolution" that ended Communist rule in the former Czechoslovakia.

The reorganization was aimed at quelling the very unrest that surfaced following the June 2009 presidential election, which many say the IRGC helped fix in favor of Ahmadinejad. During protests following the vote, members of the Basij force—dubbed "shadowy vigilantes" by Western news organizations—allegedly beat and killed opposition supporters in Tehran and other Iranian cities.

In June 2011, the United States designated the IRGC and Basij as human rights abusers under U.S. executive order 13533. A March 2013 report by a UN special rapporteur cited "widespread and systemic" torture, harassment, arrest, and attacks against human rights defenders, lawyers, and journalists. Ahead of the 2013 presidential election, opposition activists reported that IRGC forces were once again clamping down on protestors, arresting several people at a rally for Hassan Rouhani, a moderate reformist candidate.

A Money Machine

Political clout and military might are not the only attributes of today's Revolutionary Guard Corps; it is also a major financial player. The *Los Angeles Times* estimated in 2007 that the group, which was tasked with rebuilding the country after the Iran-Iraq War, now has ties to more than one hundred companies that control roughly $12 billion in construction and engineering capital, laboratories, weapons manufacturers, and companies connected to nuclear technology. IRGC has extended its influence into virtually every sector of the Iranian market. The Guards-controlled engineering firm Khatam al-Anbia, for instance, has been awarded more than 750 government contracts for infrastructure, oil, and gas projects, he says.

Looking Ahead

In recent years, analysts have differed widely on what the future holds for Iran's Revolutionary Guard Corps. Some have suggested the Guards' rising political and economic clout has put it in a position to challenge the clerical establishment. For the past thirty years, the Islamic Republic has been based on a fundamental alliance between the clergy and the Revolutionary Guards, where the clerics have been ruling the country, and the Revolutionary Guards have guarded the Islamic Republic and its values. But now the dynamic has changed to one in which the Revolutionary Guards are both ruling and guarding.

For one, the organization today is factionalized and made up of competing currents. During the Khatami era, for instance, the Guards' leadership supported conservative elements within the Iranian establishment, while the rank and file were more empathetic to the reformists. Under Ahmadinejad, splits emerged most noticeably on economic policy.

In the lead-up to the 2013 presidential election, two top candidates had links to the Guards: Mohammad Bagher Ghalibaf, who led the corps from 1997 to 2000, and Jalili, Iran's chief nuclear negotiator, who is a wounded veteran of the war with Iraq. Many Iran observers see the ascent of these two figures in presidential politics as an affirmation of the IRGC's prominence in Iran's corridors of power.

Missiles and Warheads

Iran has developed some weapons of mass destruction (WMD) programs, and it has a relatively advanced ballistic and cruise missile program. Although Iran is widely believed unlikely to use chemical or biological weapons or to transfer them to its regional proxies or allies, Iran's missiles are considered to pose a realistic and significant threat to U.S. ships, forces, and allies in the Gulf region and beyond. The April 2, 2015, framework nuclear accord makes no reference to limiting Iran's ability to develop ballistic missiles, although the tentative accord indicates that U.S. sanctions on such Iranian efforts would remain in place.

Chemical and Biological Weapons Official U.S. reports and testimony state that Iran maintains the capability to produce chemical warfare (CW) agents and "probably" has the capability to produce some biological warfare agents for offensive purposes, if it made the decision to do so. This raises questions about Iran's compliance with its obligations under the Chemical Weapons Convention (CWC), which Iran signed on January 13, 1993, and ratified on June 8, 1997.

The Administration asserts that Iran's ballistic missiles and its acquisition of indigenous production of anti-ship cruise missiles (ASCMs) provide capabilities for Iran to project power. DNI Clapper testified in February 2015, that the intelligence community assesses that "Iran's ballistic missiles are inherently capable of delivering WMD."

Tehran views its conventionally armed missiles as an integral part of its strategy to deter—and if necessary retaliate against—forces in the region, including U.S. forces. A particular worry of U.S. commanders remains Iran's inventory of cruise missiles, which can reach U.S. ships in the Gulf quickly after launch. U.S. officials and reports have estimated that Iran is steadily expanding its missile and rocket inventories and has "boosted the lethality and effectiveness of existing systems with accuracy improvements and new sub-munition payloads."

It is unclear the extent to which Iran continues to receive outside assistance for its missile program. Some reports suggest Iranian technicians may have witnessed North Korea's satellite launch in December 2012, which, if true, could support the view that Iran-North Korea missile cooperation is extensive. Table 3 contains some details on Iran's missile programs.

Iran's programs do not appear to have been significantly set back by the November 12, 2011, explosion at a ballistic missile base outside Tehran that destroyed it and killed the base commander.

Iran's Missile Arsenal

Shahab-3 ("Meteor")

The 800-mile range missile is operational, and Defense Department reports indicate Tehran has improved its lethality and effectiveness.

Shahab-3 "Variant" /Sijil/Ashoura

The Sijil, or Ashoura, is a solid fuel Shahab-3 variant with 1,200-1,500-mile range. The April 2012 DOD report indicates the missile is increasing in range, lethality, and accuracy, potentially putting large portions of the Near East and Southeastern Europe in range. In June 2011, Iran unveiled underground missile silos. BM-25 1,500-mile range. In April 2006, Israel's military intelligence chief said that Iran had received a shipment of North Korean-supplied BM-25 missiles, capable of carrying nuclear warheads. The Washington Times appeared to corroborate this reporting in a July 6, 2006, story, which asserted that the North Korean-supplied missile is based on a Soviet-era "SS-N-6" missile.

Press accounts in December 2010 indicated that Iran may have received components but not the entire BM-25 missile from North Korea. U.S. officials have long asserted that Iran might be capable of developing an intercontinental ballistic missile (3,000 mile range) by 2015. That deadline has arrived, and Iran has not announced any tests of a missile of intercontinental range. However, DNI Clapper has testified that Iran has the means and motivation to develop longer range missiles, including ICBMs.

Short Range Ballistic Missiles and Cruise Missiles

Iran is fielding increasingly capable, short range ballistic missiles, according to DOD 2012 and 2014 reports, such as ability to home in on and target ships while the missile is in flight. One version could be a short range ballistic missile named the Qiam, tested in August 2010. Iran has long worked on a 200 mile range "Fateh 110" missile (solid propellant), a version of which is the Khaliji Fars (Persian Gulf) anti-ship ballistic missile that could threaten maritime activity throughout the Persian Gulf. Iran also is able to arm its patrol boats with Chinese-made C-802 anti-ship cruise missiles. Iran also has C-802's and other missiles emplaced along Iran's coast, including the Chinese-made CSSC-2 (Silkworm) and the CSSC-3 (Seersucker). Iran also possesses a few hundred short-range ballistic missiles, including the Shahab-1 (Scud-b), the Shahab-2 (Scud-C), and the Tondar-69 (CSS-8).

Space Vehicle

In February 2009, Iran successfully launched a small, low-earth satellite on a Safir-2 rocket (range about 155 miles). The Pentagon said the launch was "clearly a concern of ours" because "there are dual-use capabilities here which could be applied toward the development of long-range missiles." A larger space vehicle, Simorgh, was displayed in February 2010, and Iran has claimed additional satellite launches since, including the launch and return of a vehicle carrying a small primate in December 2013.

Warheads

Wall Street Journal report of September 14, 2005, said that U.S. intelligence believes Iran is working to adapt the Shahab-3 to deliver a nuclear warhead. Subsequent press reports said that U.S. intelligence captured an Iranian computer in mid-20.

Asymmetric Warfare Capacity

Iran appears to be attempting to compensate for its conventional military weaknesses by developing a significant capacity for "asymmetric warfare" that would maximize Iran's advantages and minimize those of a large, advanced force like that of the United States. The unclassified executive summary of the 2014 Defense Department report on Iran's military capability says that Iran continues to develop "anti-access and area denial" capabilities to control the Strait of Hormuz and its approaches. It is developing increasingly lethal systems such as more advanced naval mines, submarines, coastal defense and anti-ship cruise and ballistic missiles, and attack craft.

The purpose of Iran threatening or trying to block the Strait could be to threaten the world economy, perhaps in order to extract concessions from the international community. It is a long-asserted core U.S. interest to preserve the free flow of oil and freedom of navigation in the Persian Gulf, which is only about 20 miles wide at its narrowest point. The Strait is identified by the Energy Information Administration as a key potential "chokepoint" for the world economy.

Each day, about 17 million barrels of oil flow through the Strait, which is 35% of all seaborne traded oil and 20% of all worldwide traded oil.37 Iran publicly stated that it was stopping or firing on several commercial shipping companies transiting the Strait in May 2015 to force a resolution of commercial disputes with the shipping companies involved, but may have been seeking to demonstrate its potential ability to control the Strait.

Were Iran to take action against the United States and the GCC states, Iranian forces would probably rely most heavily on ships, submarines, and short range missiles. Iran could potentially use its large fleet of small boats to "swarm" U.S. ships. It also has the ability to lay numerous mines in the narrow Strait of Hormuz. Iran has added naval bases along its Gulf coast in recent years, enhancing its ability to threaten shipping in the Strait. In February 2013, Iran began constructing an additional naval base near Iran's border with Pakistan, on the Sea of Oman.

Iran's Conventional Military Arsenal

Military Personnel: 420,000+. Regular army ground force is about 350,000, Revolutionary Guard Corps (IRGC) ground force is about 150,000. IRGC navy is about 20,000 and regular navy is about 18,000. Regular Air Force has about 30,000 personnel and IRGC Air Force is of unknown size – it controls Iran's strategic missile forces.

Security Forces: About 40,000-60,000 law enforcement forces on duty, with another 600,000 Basij (volunteer militia under IRGC control) available for combat or internal security missions.

Tanks: 1,650+ Includes 480 Russian-made T-72

Ships: 100+ (IRGC and regular Navy) Includes 4 Corvette; 18 IRGC-controlled Chinese-made patrol boats, several hundred small boats.) Also has 3 Kilo subs (reg. Navy controlled). 2012 DOD report says Iran may have acquired additional ships and submarines over the past two years, but does not stipulate a supplier, if any.

Midget Subs: Iran has been long said to possess several small subs, possibly purchased assembled or in kit form from North Korea. Iran claimed on November 29, 2007, to have produced a new small sub equipped with sonar-evading technology, and it claimed to deploy four Iranian-made "Ghadir class" subs to the Red Sea in June 2011.

Surface-to-Air Missiles (SAMs): 150+ I-Hawk plus possibly some Stinger

Combat Aircraft: 330+ Includes 25 MiG-29 and 30 Su-24. Still dependent on U.S. F-4's, F-5's and F-14 bought during Shah's era.

Anti-aircraft Missile Systems: Russia delivered to Iran (January 2007) 30 anti-aircraft missile systems (Tor M1), worth over $1 billion. In December 2007, Russia agreed to sell the highly capable S-300 air defense system, which would greatly enhance Iran's air defense capability, at an estimated cost of $800 million. The system would not, according to most experts, technically violate the provisions of U.N. Resolution 1929, because the system is not covered in the U.N. Registry on Conventional Arms. On September 22, 2010, then Russian

President Medvedev signed a decree banning the supply of the system to Iran, asserting that its provision to Iran is banned by Resolution 1929. In August 2011, Iran and Russia took their dispute over the non-delivery of the S-300 to the International Court of Justice. After the April 2, 2015, framework nuclear accord, Russian officials indicated they would proceed with the S-300 delivery.

Defense Budget: About 3% of GDP

Al Quds Force

An instrument of Iran's national security policy is not only to deploy conventional force but to supports armed factions in the region, some of which are named as terrorist organizations by the Iran, Gulf Security, and U.S. Policy

Some U.S. observers interpret Iran's objectives in supporting armed factions as attempting to overturn a power structure in the Middle East that Iran asserts favors the United States, Israel, and Sunni Muslim Arab regimes. However, in order not to stoke Sunni-Shiite tensions, Iran often publicly couches its support for Shiite-led movements as support for an "oppressed" underclass. The strategy helps Iran expand its influence with little direct risk, gives Tehran a measure of deniability, and serves as a "force multiplier" that compensates for a relatively weak conventional force.

Some U.S. officials have predicted that, in the event of a U.S.-Iran confrontation, Iran would try to retaliate through terrorist attacks inside the United States or against U.S. embassies and facilities in Europe or the Persian Gulf. Iran could also try to direct anti-U.S. militias in Afghanistan to attack U.S. personnel there. Iran's support for armed factions particularly Lebanese Hezbollah, formed the basis of Iran's addition to the U.S. list of state sponsors of terrorism ("terrorism list") in January 1984.

Some experts speculate that Rouhani seeks to curb Iran's support for militant movements in the region because their activities could injure his goals of broader international engagement.

However, many doubt that Rouhani would be able to do so because he is perceived as having no authority over the Qods Force commander, Qasem Soleimani, who is said to report directly to Khamene'i. Some observers assert that the gains by Sunni rebellions against pro-Iranian governments in Iraq and Syria have cast doubt within Iranian leadership circles about Soleimani's preferred policy of providing unqualified support for pro-Iranian Shiite leaders in the region.

In prior decades, Iran's conduct of international terrorism took the form of assassinating dissidents abroad. In the late 1980s and early 1990s, Iran allegedly was responsible for the assassination of several Iranian dissidents based in Europe, including Iranian Kurdish dissident leader Abdol Rahman Qasemlu, several other Kurdish leaders (*including those killed at the Mykonos café in Berlin in September 1992*), the brother of PMOI leader Masud Rajavi, and several figures close to the late Shah. In May 2010, France allowed the return to Iran of Vakili Rad, who had been convicted in the 1991 stabbing of the Shah's last prime minister, Shahpour Bakhtiar. Iran has not been accused of dissident assassinations abroad in well over a decade.

Iran is supporting a number of armed factions on several fronts in the region, as well as some regional leaders who the United States has said need to leave office.

Lebanese Hezbollah

Lebanese Hezbollah, which is named by the United States as a Foreign Terrorist Organization (FTO), is Iran's chief protégé movement in the region by virtue of a long relationship that began when Lebanese Shiite clerics of the pro-Iranian Lebanese Da'wa Party began to organize in 1982, after Israel's invasion that year. Iran's political, financial, and military aid to Hezbollah has helped it become a major force in Lebanon's politics, and Iran reportedly was instrumental in persuading Hezbollah leaders to become directly involved in the Syria conflict on behalf of Syrian President Bashar Al Assad.

Recent State Department terrorism reports assert that Iran "has provided hundreds of millions of dollars in support of Hezbollah and has trained thousands of Hezbollah fighters at camps in Iran." Israeli sources report that Iran has given Hezbollah about 100,000 rockets of varying types since the Israel-Hezbollah War in 2006, some of which can reach virtually all parts of Israel.

Hamas

The State Department annual report on terrorism has consistently stated that Iran supplies funding, weapons, and training to Hamas, a Sunni Islamist Palestinian organization which is named as an FTO. Hamas has exercised control in the Gaza Strip since seizing that territory in a civil conflict with the non-Islamist Fatah organization, which dominates the Palestinian Authority based in the West Bank. Hamas opposed the efforts by Assad to defeat the rebellion militarily and a rift opened with Assad and with Iran. Iran has since sought to rebuild the Hamas relationship by reportedly providing missile technology and other equipment.

Iraq

The June 2014 offensive led by the Islamic State organization threatened Iraq's government and Iran responded quickly by supplying IRGC-QF advisers, intelligence drone surveillance, weapons shipments, and other assistance. The IRGC-QF advisers have helped reactivate the Shiite militias as a core of armed support to the faltering Iraq Security Forces.

The United States also supports the Iraqi government but cautions that the government reliance on Shiite militias will hinder efforts at political reconciliation that are needed to defeat the Islamic State in Iraq. The Shiite militias include As'aib Ahl Al Haq (League of the Righteous), Kata'ib Hezbollah (Hezbollah Brigades), and the Mahdi Army of Moqtada Al Sadr (renamed the Peace Brigades in 2014). Kata'ib Hezbollah has been named a Foreign Terrorist Organization (FTO) by the United States.

Syria

In Syria, President Bashar Al Assad has been Iran's closest Arab ally, whereas the United States has called for Assad to leave office. Syria has been the main transit point for Iranian weapons shipments to Hezbollah, and both Iran and Syria have used Hezbollah as leverage against Israel to try to achieve regional and territorial aims. In an effort to prevent Assad's downfall—and the likely accession of a regime run by Sunni Islamists - Iran is providing substantial amounts of material support to the Syrian regime, including funds, weapons, and fighters.

Many accounts indicate that Iran has IRGC-QF personnel to Syria to advise the regime and fight alongside the Syrian military. International and U.S. officials reportedly seek to persuade Iran to abandon Assad, presumably in favor of a figure that Iran would perceive as not inimical to its interests—such as the securing of a weapons supply corridor to Hezbollah.

Houthi

Rebels in Yemen. Iran has been supporting a Zaydi Shiite revivalist movement known as the "Houthis" with unknown quantities of arms and other aid, reportedly including AK-47s, rocket-propelled grenades, and other arms. A senior Iranian official reportedly told journalists in December 2014 that the Qods Force has a "few hundred" personnel in Yemen training Houthi fighters.41 In September 2014, the Houthis seized major locations in the capital, Sanaa, and took control of major government locations in January 2015, forcing Saleh's successor, Abd Rabu Mansur Al Hadi, to flee to Aden.

Some observers have argued that the Houthis' successes—including advancing into Aden by April 2015 despite bombing by a Saudi-led coalition of Arab states—might demonstrate Iran's continuing ability to project influence in the Arabian Peninsula and the broader Middle East. However, others counter that Iran's support for the Houthis does not appear to be nearly as significant as its aid to closer allies like Lebanese Hezbollah.